Collecting Luxury Watches

Leonard Lowe

2016-06-18

Testimonials

5/5 Stars ***** Great book for watch enthusiasts! This is the second e-book from this author, that I've read. He has a nice, clear writing style and definitely he has lots of insight on what makes a particular watch brand and watch model valuable. I thought the omission of Grand Seiko was somewhat odd, but it is still a great book.« (July 18, 2017)

The Book

Leonard Lowe wrote three books about luxury watches: Luxury Watches, Rolex Watches and Ten Fun Things to do with Luxury Watches. And here is his fourth one, his most personal one, with the most insight in his own personal collection and his thoughts why and when he purchased his collectibles. A personal history of becoming a watch enthusiast despite starting out an ordinary person with a lot of hints and thoughts on purchasing and collecting luxury watches.

»I never decided to be a watch collector. It just happened somehow. This book finally tells the story of my passion for luxury watches, how I learned about them, what I considered before and after purchasing my pieces and how it is owning and wearing them. I am sure a lot of my considerations will help the new and even the advanced watch lover to learn even more about watches, about collecting them or – if you're not a collector – just about finding the right one-and-only watch for your wrist. What you will find in this ebook is an amusing, entertaining and insightful story of my personal experiences with luxury watches. Have fun...!«

Join Leonard Lowe on his journey through the world of luxury watches and find a lot of useful and inspiring insights about this compelling hobby.

The Author

Leonard Lowe is a german engineer, scientific researcher and professor for mechanical engineering. Throughout his career his success formula was always 'never believe, always question – never stand still, always learn – never accept, always understand'.

He is the author of several books on technology, nature, philosophy, history and politics.

Beyond his professional live he is a tech and hi-tech enthusiast, computer geek, brilliant thinker and writer. He loves to acquire knowledge and share it. His sharp analyses and unusual views help his readers making the right decisions in many different areas of life.

Online Book Stores

Books from THINK-eBooks are available at
http://think-ebooks.com/where-to-buy/

Leonard Lowe has written the following books:

- Collecting Luxury Watches

- Ten Fun Things to do with Luxury Watches

- Rolex Watches

- Luxury Watches – A Purchasing Guide

- Why Mac OS – Why A Mac?

- The ONE Solution to all of your R&D Problems

Imprint

We thank Rolex S.A., Patek Philippe S.A., Audemars Piguet S.A., Breitling S.A., Panerai S.A., Omega S.A., Hublot S.A. IWC S.A., Jaeger-LeCoultre S.A., Eterna S.A., and A. Lange AG for their kind support.

Contents

8 CONTENTS

Chapter 0

Foreword

Every watch enthusiast and beginning collector probably goes through the same process – more or less. So here I share my thoughts and experiences over the years and how the watch 'virus' caught me. Perhaps it is a bit like Herpes: you don't need to be infected in the first place. The virus is just always there, it only needs a button pressed to be released. The passion is always there, you just need to discover it for yourself.

In the beginning I was in my teens and I wanted an Omega Speedmaster – well sort of. I wanted a chronograph and 'Speedmaster' sounded quite cool in my ears. But I didn't take this idea quite seriously, because I found out that such a watch was simply way too expensive. And I did not know which of the many available models zu choose. I did not know anything about luxury watches or Swiss made watches, so I just walked away from the idea.

And back then I thought that a decent watch was first of all one featuring all that pcak technology, like quartz, solar, digital-analogue, radio-controlled.

So I never would have chosen the right Speedmaster, the one with the plastic crystal. And being accustomed to endlessly running quartz watches, I of course would never have chosen one with a hand wound movement. So in short it was a good decision to not buy back then because I for sure had bought the *wrong* one. Booop.

But I knew I wanted one and I also knew why: of course because it was a chronograph. Every boy or young man wants a chronograph... just because he needs a chronograph. A chronograph is meant to measure time precisely, e.g. if you are racing or running or competing in any other way. And because being a young man is all about competing and running, you of course need a chronograph to symbolize that.

That way the chronograph complication was the first complication that caught my eye, partly also because I could not imagine why someone would make a fuzz out of a date window and consider a date function a 'complication'. Showing the date wasn't what I could imagine being complicated so a 'complication' of that nature wasn't anything I accepted. What I could accept was a chronograph complication. Please remember: my first watch would be a quartz watch. The date wasn't of my concern at all. But a chrono would have been so cool.

A chronograph was cool, because it had additional registers on the dial and it also had these magical two (start/stop and reset) buttons that made the watch even more significant and busy and important... and competitive. Every boy needs a chronograph.

But it took the boy another 25 years to finally get it.

My Collection

How many pieces do I have?

8.

What? Only 8? Is this already a collection worth writing about?

Yes, I think it is.

The quality and appeal of a collection has nothing to do with quantity but everything with quality. If you have 5 quality pieces, you already have more of a collection than one who has 100 worthless watches. Of course, you may both call a collection, but they are it in the same way, as you can have a collection of 5 diamonds of 150 empty cans of Coke.

So with at this time 4 Rolex watches, 2 Omegas, 1 Panerai and

1 Eterna, it is indeed also a rather balanced collection mainly of sports watches. And that is not so bad at all. But the fascinating stories lay the details: the stories behind the watches, their history, their heritage, the manufacturers, the technological innovation, the ideas and visions, finally, the applications and the sometimes rather famous bearers of these watches.

Your benefit, reading about that, might also be found in the considerations that led me to each individual purchase, which you might want to consider also, when you buy a similar or even the very same watch. It even might be amusing and entertaining to learn how a individual purchase might be carried out. You probably will learn about the watch and the reasons to buy it or to stay away from it or its siblings by reading about my discoveries and decisions on my way to the purchase.

That is the intellectual riches behind every watch collection and with this their idealistic worth also building up parts of also its monetary value.

Advantages of Watch Collecting

The best thing about collecting luxury watches is that you can enjoy your hobby all day long – often without the people around you even noticing! You can enjoy it any time you like. As often as necessary. Even throughout working hours.

That distinguishes this elite hobby clearly from all the other similarly reasonable hobbies, like hunting just one ball together with another 21 guys on some gras, or chatting on Whatsapp or wearing your underwear ontop of your cloths.

You can enjoy wearing your luxury watches, without anyone noticing. How? Easy: you wear them just you would wear any ordinary watch. You most of the time even pretend that it is a normal watch.

What is of course ridiculous: no Seiko, no Citizen, no Casio (sorry Japanese, you make great watches!), but none of these will ever be able to make you feel like a king, like a winner, like someone precious, like a man, just by wearing it. But a Rolex does. To feel like being the crown, just wear a crown.

So, in order to enjoy your Rolex, you do pretend it being an ordinary watch, but deep in your heart you sincerely know that it of course isn't. And even this little secret is part of the magic and joy: you know, you are different and you don't even need to tell anyone. It's just there. On your wrist. Your little obscene secret.

If you want to look at your beloved watch, what of course is another important part of the fun, you just pretend looking up the time. And that's it. You have all the fun in your life, looking at one of your collectible beauties and nobody has a clue, what's going on.

Looking at it, you can for some precious moments depart into a better world, a world of perfection, luxury, beauty, exclusiveness and the true meaning of life, – and all that right in the middle of any extensive monologue on shoes of the one woman in your life, or any given business meeting with the one boss in your life, or whatever situation makes you usually on a daily basis wish being one of Saturns satellites.

And all that without anyone noticing, if, yes of course *if* only you consider these simple, essential, world exclusive rules of luxury watch owning (strictly):

1. Don't adore your watch longer than 60 sec at a time. People will think you want to signal them some kind of hidden message by your strange behavior and will pick their ears or blink at you with their eyes to let you know, they understood.

2. If someone asks what time it is after you looked at your watch for some extended period, you better know. We luxury watch aficionados know, sometimes it is hard, to look up the time, smitten with the beauty of your timepiece. You look at it – and you look at it – and you really don't care about the position of those utterly beautiful, elegant, whitegold, slightly green shimmering hands that so gracefully... where was I? What-do-ya-mean by, what time? How shall I know?

3. Openly looking at your watch is in a lot of cultures considered rude, because it expresses the wish to be in another place soon: so, look at your watch secretly, e.g. under the table – in which

case you can forget rule No 1, because everyone will think, you fell asleep and will eventually quietly leave the room.

4. Never ever tell anyone the thing you look at is 'a Rolex'. Better say Patek-Philippe, because nobody will know, or even better Audemars-Piguet, what nobody will even try to repeat and pronounce. They will just want one thing: forget that intimidating situation quickly. They will feel like you just told them you have a Ferrari and they never heard of Ferrari before – what is basically exactly what happened. If on the other hand you do the wrong thing and say 'a Rolex', your salary will be reduced and your company car will be replaced by the smallest one available. Only exception to the rule: you own the company.

5. If someone asks you, what operating system your smartwatch runs on, say, the latest version and nod knowingly.

6. From time to time talk to your watch, so that everybody thinks it is just a smartwatch with a fancy custom watch face.

7. If anyone presses you to tell todays weather forecast or the stock market from your smartwatch, pretend the bluetooth connect to you phone has just broken down. Instead, offer him the exact time. He won't notice that it might be off plus or minus 2 seconds. If he indeed does, tell him you need to configure the internet time server synchronisation anytime soon.

8. Always wear just one of your watches at a time. Two is unnecessary, as luxury watches are very reliable. Note than three are ridiculous for the lack of another wrist. And of course you never wear all of them unless you are an Octopus.

Chapter 1

Liking Watches

I always was a technical guy. As a kid I of course liked fast cars, hifi stereos and every kind of high tech gadget you could get in the 1970s and 1980s – which weren't so many compared to today. So my fascination for those little perfectionist machines inside mechanical watches is not quite incidental.

The tradition says that you are considered a person in your own right, when you are accepted by the community. In my case, being a protestant christian that happened when I was 14 years old and the tradition also was that you get a decent watch at that occasion – besides all the religious stuff; and being just a christian luckily nobody tried to cut something off from me.

So being accepted as an individual by my community, I got a 'rather decent' watch: a Citizen Digi-Ana, a quartz watch with steel case and bracelet and a white analog dial – to replace my cheap noname 'Meisteranker' quartz watch I wore before. A watch that as I learned, at least was made in Glashütte (!!), being in the German Democratic Republic back then and being made by the communist German slave workers there to sell it to clueless West-Germans like me, who took it 30 years to find out the real origin of those quite reasonably priced watches.

The Citizen Digi-Ana was at least made in Japan and its analog dial was accompanied by a smaller digital lcd dial that could do all the tricks and magic that a watch in the mid 1980 had

Figure 1.1: becoming of age: Citizen DigiAna from 1985

to do: chronograph (bip,... bip), countdown (beep beep beep), two alarms (beep), hour alarm (beep) – and a date complication (without beep).

Figure 1.2: not a Patek but precious to me: Citizen DigiAna

In the beginning I of course only wore that Citizen like it was a Patek. I wore it only on sundays and at family celebrations. But that changed some years later. In a fast – only a little too fast – curve, the front wheel of my bike slid on some sand, I lost control over the bike completely and really unpleasently touched the ground with my knees, hands and wrists first – and my cheap everyday digital quartz watch – that was indeed made in Glashütte for gods sake! – got some really serious scratches across and all over the case and the glas (which of course was no mineral glas or sapphire) and was basically close to unusable. So I switched to the Citizen and from that day on, wore if for about 10 years nearly every day. And it did what it was supposed to do and still works today. And as my bike skills improved also, it, still to this day, has no scratches at all.

Figure 1.3: not of the same kind, but clearly inspired: Citizen DigiAna and AP Royal Oak

When I look at it today, I think it somehow seems to be inspired by the Royal Oak design. It is not really square in shape but also not really round. It has that edged bezel with 8 edges and the integrated bracelet much like the Royal Oak. And I think it is still a good looking watch today and the digital part of the design is not so obnoxious as it is with other models of that era where the little LCD display is placed above the analogue dial. It still works today as a dresswatch and I use it from time to time if I want something really decent and rugged.

Chapter 2

My First Decent Watch

Now I was an adult with a diploma and now I wanted a 'real' watch. It should represent my status – at least a little bit, because my status still wasn't so impressive at all.

There are a lot of ways to become mature and one of it is to graduate from university. And of course this was another occation to get a decent watch. This time I took the question which watch to choose more seriously. Being an engineer now I had my ways to find out which technical product was not only appropriate by its looks, but also technologically, regarding quality and all that. So I looked which brands would be there and what watches they had to offer.

A fellow student at that time told me about the difference between watchmakers and real watch manufacturers (as he put it). He defined it like this: the first ones all use the same movements from a standard movement supplier and merely design cases and bracelets, but not the heart of the matter: the movement; while the latter ones make their own movements, and everything else by themselves – what he of course considered to be much better. And he told me that in the huge amount of watchmakers only a view actually made their own movements. I remember him mentioning Rolex (of course), and Zenith – and some other with rather peculiar names that I could not recall seconds after I heard them. Today I would reconstruct them to have been: Jaeger-LeCoultre, Audemars-

Piguet, Patek-Philippe and Vacheron Constantin and perhaps Breguet. You might guess why I couldn't recall them in the first place.

Inhouse Movements

So as I learned the idea is that the watch making world is divided up into to parts: one, the manufacturers who make the whole watch themselves, especially the movement; two, the watchmakers who make the case and the bracelet but get the movement from ETA. The first ones are highly respected, the others try to catch up. The first ones are just a few, the others are hundreds.

For that reason, participants of the second section try to become one of the manufacturers simply by also making their own movements.

Today Omega and Breitling, Panerai and Hublot and many others try to make their own inhouse movements to become one of the more respected manufacturers. But in my humble opinion that is a complete missunderstanding. This will not help anything, it indeed makes things worse. And here is why:

Think about it: e.g. what Rolex does. Rolex is one of the true manufacturers who (today) only sells watches with their own inhouse made movements inside. But this is not the important part. The important part is the outstanding quality of these movements and their technical perfection, especially their reliability and highly precise timekeeping. Even Rolex would not be able to reach this level of quality using ETA movements, however they would alter them. And for that reason, Rolex does not only make their own movements. They indeed control the whole manufacturing chain from the very beginning. They make literally their own steel in their own foundary. They cast their own gold, platinum and other materials from raw material. And then they begin making that into movements, dials, hands, cases and bracelets. By that they reach perfection.

The goal is not making their own movements. The goal is perfection. And the way Rolex tries to reach that is by making absolutely everything themselves.

The misunderstanding is that if Breitling or Omega, Hublot or Panerai make their own movements, they would be on the same level as Rolex. But that's far from the truth. They still don't play in the same league with Rolex or Jaeger-LeCoultre, because making their own movements is not the goal, it is only the way to eventualy reach the goal. The goal is making the perfect watch. And the most importand step to reach this, is making *perfect* movements, very very good movements. The goal is not making some movement, but the perfect movement. And that is the difference and the misunderstanding.

I will not say that the inhouse movements of Breitling and Omega, Hublot and Panerai are bad movements. But it does not make these companies any better than before if they now make their own movements. What would make them part of High Horology would be the reputation of perfect watchmaking. Just making their own movements doesn't improve anything.

Indeed it can be a step back from using ETA movements. ETA movements are not bad at all. Indeed they are considered very reliable and rugged. At least ETA is without question the top volume seller of Swiss watch movements. Of course they are also very basic and simple, but they are not bad indeed. A lot of famous watches of the 1980s and 1990s like the Omega Seamaster Professinal or the whole Panerai model range are all based on pimped ETA movements. And they do their work flawlessly in millions of watches.

Today Panerai makes more and more inhouse calibers and you can hear more and more quality complaints of every kind. This is not an improvement and that way they will not close up to Rolex or JLC or any other top brand at all.

Only Mechanical Watches, please

My collegue from University also told me that only a mechanical watch is a real watch worth mentioning and that a quartz watch is not considered any good in the luxury watch segment. Ok. I did not know that, but it sounded reasonable and so I knew roughly where to look for my own 'real' watch.

I quickly found out that there was of course Breitling (lots of chronographs), but which I found were too expensive at that time with some watches for over 6.000 or even 8.000 Deutsche Mark (these were the good old times, when we had a currency that actually worked!) and the Breitling models also back then were often already 44 mm in diameter, so I also thought they were to big for my writst (I was 29 years old, 191 cm in height but brought only 80kgs to the scales, and I also wasn't exactly the muscular type, so my wrists were rather thin). Too thin for a Breitling Chronomat or a big fellow like that.

Of course I considered the Speedmaster. But still, I could not find one that fit my vision. The original one seemed very black and a bit dull to me and I did not trust the other, more colorful ones to be the real thing either.

Figure 2.1: first alternatives: Omega Speedmaster Automatic, Omega Seamaster Chrono Titanium Gold, Omega Constellation

The first watch that caught my eye was then the Omega Seamaster Chronograph Titanium-Gold. I just liked the look of it. But unfortunately I then found out that this thing was also like the Breitling chronos something like unbelievable 8.000 DM (what would be at least 8.000 EUR today). And so this idea also was over very quickly.

Also the Speedmaster was more expensive than e.g. the normal

Omega Seamaster (without the chronograph, the gold and the titanium). And then I thought, ok, what do I need a chronograph for? And I decided for a three-hand watch with a date. And that's it.

For some time I considered the Omega Constellation, but in the end that one also did not satisfy me, it was not cool, not really. It tended to be more elegant than sporty, but man!, I was 29!

So I searched on. I looked at the model ranges of Tag Heuer and Longines as I of course knew these brands from the sports events on TV when these guys took the time at skiing and racing and all that stuff. But they also did not have just one model that I really liked. Everything they had looked a bit like the copy of a copy of some (to me at that time) invisible and unknown original. It just completely escped my thoughts that I had to look to Rolex to find that original. But as I had decided to not buy anything less than the coolest watch on the market I was rather critical and had to continue my search.

I of course knew Rolex. But I never considered it. Back then I estimated a Rolex being simply way too expensive and for me completely out of range. The image I had of that brand was that it was playing on a completely different level than I considered myself in. A Rolex was a watch for a really rich person, for someone who earned a real ****load of money – and obviously not for a young engineer like me who had not earned any own money in his life so far.

Then I found out that Omega seemed to be a rather good combination of quality and decent reputation while being rather reasonably priced (at least compared to Breitling and Rolex). Also Omega seemed to me a valuable brand with a good name that wouldn't be forgotten tomorrow. That Omega was indeed number two behind Rolex in the luxury watches market I did not know, as I did not know that there was a high horology segment and above that the Holy Trinity of watchmakers. But I somehow felt that Omega wasn't the worst bet.

Finally I narrowed my choice down to the Omega Constellation and the Omega Seamaster Professional. And despite the James

Figure 2.2: what a great watch: Omega Seamaster Professional Ref. 2531.8000 (1999)

Bond connection that I felt was more embarrassing than cool, I chose the Seamaster, simply because I felt that I had reached my goal of finding the most beautiful watch on the market.

I got it for 2.500 DM back then and what a good choice that was! To this very day for some 15+ years now I wear it with absolute pleasure.

To be quite correct as I already told you, I did not purchase it myself but got it as a present for my university degree.

Owning It, Wearing It

The Seamaster wears like a charm. All the surfaces that touch your skin are exceptionally well finished and although it weighs 167 real steel gramms at 41 mm case diameter, you nearly don't feel it on the wrist and it absolutely never bothers you whatsoever.

You can pull this watch off with a suit, a bathing suit, a T-shirt or whatever you want: it always fits. It slides like a charm under each cuff and will never ever go on your nerves. It just sits there on your wrist and looks great.

The Omega Seamaster Professional is a in every conceivable way perfectly balanced watch. It is a diver and a sports watch, but you can perfectly wear it as a dress watch, as it is quite slim

Figure 2.3: real classic: Omega Seamaster Professional (1999)

and elegant. It is not that outstandingly light on the wrist, but it is so well balanced with the bracelet that you can wear it all day with ease and joy and it indeed wears (nearly) as much as perfect as the Rolex Yachtmaster. It has some bling to it, as the bracelet is of outstanding beauty, but not so much, that it wasn't a decent watch any more. It is not a black on black watch. It has some color, but the blue of the bezel and the dial is so well balanced that it is just blue enough to be not dark and decent enough to not be too colorful. The structure of the dial is just decent enough to be cool. The waves remind you that it is a diving watch, but it is decent enough to not being dull. The readability of the dial, the hands and the date is just superb. White hour markers and hands against a dark blue background is perfectly readable in almost every lighting situation. And finally the movement and the price of this package is just outstanding: really good quality for a very low price of $2000. That is what I call a classic and perfectly balanced.

I obviously was right that this was one of the best looking watches in the market, as that particular model from 1999 is still today, 15+ years later, considered being one of the true classics from that era.

An even Important Model

And as I later found out, that watch really had a serious and even important impact on the luxury watch market: At that time Rolex, of course already the top brand in the market, sold models that, to be positive, focused on function and reliability and not so much on the look and feel. Their top models from that era, the Submariner, the Explorer II and the GMT Master II especially all had the Rolex Oyster bracelet with the hollow links, the so called 'rattlesnake' bracelet. That bracelet earned its name because of the peculiar noise it makes when you shake it. It makes sounds and feels like it was hollow,... well, just because it is. And the problem with that is, that 'hollow' is not exactly something that in any way, shape or form fits, what you expect from a $6.000 luxury watch.

That is of course: although the hollow links totally make sense. A watch sits on your wrist the whole day. So despite this has absolutely nothing to do with showing the right time in the first place, it should also wear with comfort – and if you go another step further, also with ellegance. And comfort has a lot to do with weight. And weight comes from the watch itself and... the bracelet. So you either wear the watch on a leather strap, which is not recommended for a diving watch, as the water will kill the leather, or you wear it on a metal bracelet... and that is usually quite heavy.

What is the solution to that issue: make the links hollow and save weight. Something everybody in the aerospace industry would recommend. These guys do this all day: making things light by making them hollow. And this is what Rolex obviously chose to do making serious tool watches for a luxury price tag: a hollow rattlesnake bracelet.

And then came the Seamaster. Not only that Omega 'stole' the James Bond connection from Rolex (because originally in the Ian Flemming novels, 007 wore a Rolex Explorer, like his author, and later, in the movies Sean Connery wore a Rolex Submariner), now with the Seamaster they also offered a watch of such quality, with a especially well made high class bracelet, a very good clasp and a pretty case, that you almost forgot that it was not powered by one of those rugged 100-year lifetime Rolex movements, but 'just' by a standard ETA movement, which was of course 'optimized' by Omega making it totally their own.

Now, the Seamaster sold so well, that Rolex had to struggle. They develped and released their own all new, massive Oyster bracelet and the all new milled out clasp as a reaction to that brillant Seamaster model.

The Seamaster became a classic and I had one, mainly because my amateurish choise was good.

The Purchase

Of course I went to an official Omega dealer to purchase the watch. To be very accurate, as I said, I got this as a present, but I could say, which watch it should be, so it was the best of both worlds: I got exactly what I wanted but I got it as a present.

So I cannot say a lot about the purchasing experience, as I wasn't there at the time. But in times before the internet, nobody would thought about another way of purchasing a luxury watch. There was no chrono24 or other internet portals that would have made it possible to compare prices between dealers in Munich, in New York and in Bangkok. There was a price list and if you asked very friendly, you got 10% off. And that was that.

Service

After about 15 years of near daily use, the power reserve of the Omega/ETA movement in the Seamaster had dropped to about 12 hours or so and winding the watch manually made a ugly metallic screeching noise so I finally decided to let it service. And spending some hundred bucks after 15 years did not seem a big investment to me.

Unfortunately I read about a watch that Omega lost. In an internet-forum I read about a guy who gave his collectible Omega watch to be serviced at Omega in Switzerland and he wrote it got lost, he never got it back and was very unhappy about that. He did not get his collectible watch back and Omega offered him a new Seamaster instead. What a rip-off.

Figure 2.4: readability still perfect in low light: Omega Seamaster Professional (1999)

So even though I basically trust the swiss guys and especially those precision guys at the watchmakers, that did not make me confident to send my watch to Switzerland and I decided to let it service by a local watch dealer with an Omega certificate.

That mostly turned out ok. The watch looked as good as new from the outside, it had been polished very carefully and only in the places where it was necessary (basically the clasp) and the noises of the movement were gone – winding it was again as soft as butter (though there still is a significant difference between winding a Rolex movement to winding an ETA).

However the power reserve did not improve a lot. It had been 12 hours before the service and about 20 hours after it at best. If this is the case because the power spring of the watch had to be replaced by a new one but the service guy had no replacement parts available since Omega keeps them to themselves I do not know.

Weaknesses

The only weakness I can think of, is scratch the resistance of the clasp. If you use it daily, the clasp collects scratches from day one and soon looks a bit worn.

And the other thing is power reserve: after 17 years of use the power reserve of the ETA movement Omega uses had dropped to a low of about 20 hours from the original 36. And this did not improve even after I had it serviced. But it still keeps time correctly so far.

So would I have the Seamaster Professional again? Yes, of course. For only 2500 bucks back in 1999 it is a fabulous watch. It is a classic today and still a beauty to look at on the wrist. I consider it a design that will still look great in another 20 years or so.

Chapter 3

My First Rolex

How an Apple Watch shapeshifted into a Rolex. I can't deny – and I don't even try to – I am an Apple enthusiast.

Not the Apple Watch

In my case the Apple watch started something that the guys from Cupertino obviously hadn't in mind.

It all began with my wife trying to buy me an Apple watch. But the result was 1. there wasn't one available, as it was not on the market back then and 2. when she told me, I said that this was a good thing that she didn't get one because frankly, I did not really want one. Instead I told her that, talking about watches, I perhaps wanted another 'real' watch to accompany my Omega Seamaster, this time perhaps a Rolex. And she said, recklessly: »if you want a Rolex, why don't you get one?«

But this was not an easy one. So to get back into my old hobby, I first compiled my old watches – to see what I had and move on from there.

But as we already saw, there wasn't so much to mention. I had a Omega Seamaster for around 1000 bucks and some basically at best mid-range stuff for some hundred bucks each. Nothing to be mentioned at all. So I had the oportunity to more or less start from scratch.

Before the Purchase

The first one is always the hardest.

I had decided that my new watch would probably be a Rolex, my first Rolex. And it obviously had to be the right model. And to choose the right one took some time. Firstly, because I had to find out which models there were. I did not know very much about Rolex back then. Secondly, because I had to find out not only what each model looked like – what you can find out on the Internet, but also what it would look like on the wrist – what you can find best on Pinterest and Google Pictures on the Internet, but also what it looked like on *my very own* wrist – what you can only find out with yourself at the dealer's, and finally what it looked like live and in reality – what you only can find out with your own eyes. And that simply takes some time, dedication and effort, escpecially as you will find out that there isn't always every Rolex in stock, even not at a official Rolex dealer. So often you go there to see two or three models and you are lucky if the dealer has at least one of them to show you.

The first Rolex models you hear about are of course the Submariner and the Daytona. But I did not like either of them, because the Sub has the stain that it is said that basically 'everybody has one'. Which in truth does not need to be true, but the *design* of the Sub, the black diving bezel and the black dial is copied so much that it at least *seems* that a lot of guy have a Sub on their wrist – even though it might be a Casio Diver or another similar thing.

My first shot aimed at three possible models, I was interested in: the GMT Master II Pepsi, the Sea-Dweller Deep Sea with the James Cameron deep blue dial and the Daytona in steel with the white dial. So I went to a really big dealer, to have a look at these watches – I obviously had not the slightest clue, that I would only make the dealer laugh.

Funny thing. The Daytona was not in stock and wasn't available for another ten years or so. What? Ten YEARS? Yes, said the clerk, they had a waiting list, from here to the moon. Oh, great

Figure 3.1: not available: Rolex Daytona, Deep Sea, GMT Pepsi Steel

teapot! Ok then: how about the Deep Sea (I did not mention the blue dial as something seemed to tell me that this special edition model wouldn't be in stock). But that didn't help much, the regular one wasn't either. And to be honest, said the clerk, it is a bit large, wink wink. Ok then,... The GMT? (I meanwhile had totally given up mentioning any specification requirements hoping this would increase I probability that I would see any watch live at that day) We have that one, he said – but not the Pepsi obviously, as this one is not available in steel at the moment. Ok, I said, then just show me whatever you have.

So that day I did not see the Pepsi, not the Daytona or the Deep Sea. At least I could put the GMT 216710 with the black bezel on my wrist, as well as the recommenadtion of the clerk: an Explorer 214270 which is the 39 mm version. This was a great model for beginners, he said.

I didn't like to be called a *beginner*. I already had an Omega Seamaster, man! So the Ex was out. Beginner. Pfff.

But all that didn't matter so much. What I, wearing an Omega Seamaster Professional for nearly 15 years, recognized instantly, was that Rolex was playing in a totally different league. This watch, the Explorer as well as the GMT was unbelivably refined, perfect in every detail, blinking and impressing me. Even if I did

Figure 3.2: try these: Rolex GMT Master II Black, Explorer: they are available

not like the GMT (the 216710!) so much, it was so obvious to me why my Seamaster had been around 2500 bucks back in the day and this fellow was and easy $7000. A whole different experience. I liked the Explorer a bit more than the GMT, but found it too harmless, to distinguished, not sporty enough. I obviously had a lot to learn.

I later that day went to another dealer to check out a TAG Heuer Carrera – and I couldn't stand that one on my wrist for more than some seconds, because compared to the Rolex models the TAG felt like made from cheap tin. It felt like garbage with razor-sharp undefined and crudely cut edges that would cut my skin any time soon. What a difference! Sorry TAG.

I for some time also considered some other watches, like the Omega Dark Side of the Moon, the Explorer II with the white dial, I went back and forth to the Explorer I and to the Daytona. But there was something wrong with the Explorer I (the Ref. 214270) recent model. It was large and sporty, but somehow I found it too decent. Beats me! It just did not speak to me. For a really masculine model I found it too decent and not sporty enough, but too sporty as a dress watch (what I basically did not want in the first place).

With the Daytona the thing was more simple: I just bought into

Figure 3.3: more options: Omega Speedmaster Dark Side of the Moon, Rolex Explorer II polar, TAG Heuer Carrera Calibre 5

the myth of the 10-years waiting list and found it too expensive at the same time. And I trusted the whole watch market too much. So I wasn't convinced at all that I should buy a new or used Daytona for around $10000 over the internet. No way. So I dropped the Daytona.

When I think about it today of course, after the 2016 Daytona model change and the subsequent jump of the Daytona prices from around $10000 to about $15000 within just some months – and that is the steel version! – I probably should have taken a used Daytona into account more seriously.

There obviously was another icon in the Rolex range. the GMT. But it was hard to find the 'right' one. The new one (the Ref. 116710) wasn't so pretty, I thought. The immense (ceramic) bezel made it look broad and heavy and the large markers on the only 40 mm case dial made it look crammed and not so elegant. I knew there was a better GMT, but it took me some time to figure out which one it was. And so the GMT wasn't obviously the one to begin with as I probably had to buy *my* GMT used. And that was a job for me to do later.

Then two things helped me: firstly, I decided that for me Rolex was not a very distinguished brand, although they also could do this business dresswatch thing very well. I decided that for me Rolex was a bit like Porsche. Loud and brutal and excellent. So my watch would be like that.

Figure 3.4: next choices: Rolex Explorer II, Rolex GMT Master II Batman, Omega Speedmaster 57

I wasn't convinced. So I looked at some more watches. I considered the Omega Speedmaster 57, but I felt it was too thick. For some time I fancied the Omega Speedmaster Dark Side of the Moon, but it also didn't convince me in the end. Then I considered the Rolex GMT Master II BLNR, the Batman. But to be honest I didn't like it either and still do (what might be a mistake), because of the Supercase that doesn't help the new 6-digit, ceramic GMT in terms of elegance. Back then I only felt that I did not like it. It wasn't perfect...

It was a tough decision.

But the simple truth is: you can't avoid the Sub. Meanwhile I have two even if they have different names. So I looked a bit deeper into the Submariner-'Family'.

I read an article about the three Rolex diving siblings: the Submariner, the Sea-Dweller 4000 and the Deep Sea. And then finally I understood. The Sub was a brillant watch but it had a problem: 1) everybody had one and 2) it had that cyclops thing. 3) It simply wasn't special enough. The Deep Sea was brillant and scarce, but it was too eccentric, too heavy, too big, too much in simply every aspect.

But there was the Sea-Dweller! The Sea-Dweller, hm? Is that the solution? The Sub that isn't a Sub, the Deep Sea that is not so immense, the perfect diver, the perfect Rolex: the Sea-Dweller 116600?

Figure 3.5: and the winner is: Rolex Sea-Dweller 4000

I had overseen this one, not understanding what it was and for what purpose and how it exactly differed from the other two. But now I understood: it was the sweet spot I was looking for. With a 40 mm case it was perfectly sized. But it was more masculine than the Sub. It had no cyclops lense on the crystal and it looked quite perfect. Even the (as I later found out) Super-Case and the Maxi-Dial were quite perfect for it as it could stand these rougher geometries well – compared to all the other Rolex models that more or less suffer from that change. It could handle these design changes Rolex applied to its whole product range in the late 2000s damaging the look of nearly every model, what partly caused the vintage movement. But the Sea-Dweller was the only model that could 'wear' this new look, and make it look cool!

It basically was a Sub, but more than that, a modernized, better, louder, more brutal and masculine and at the same time absolutely brillant variation of the already brillant Sub. It was everything the Sub ever was, and more.

It was the sweet spot in between the large Deep Sea, the cyclops eyed Sub and the dateless Sub. It resembles the classic Submariner

nodate like no other Rolex diver does, because it has no cyclops lens
and for that reason looks as balanced as the original Submariner
ever did. It had everything you need and I wanted. I had found
my first Rolex.

Purchasing it

You see, I am not rich. When I think about buying something
for more than $5000, it is not that I don't feel the money. And
if that is the case – like for most watch enthusiasts – you want
something right for the money you pay, you want something flawless,
something perfect – probably something virginal.

Your *first* Rolex or any other top notch luxury watch must
inevitably be one thing: perfect. So when you purchase your first
luxury watch, you inevitably purchase a new retail watch.

Because obviously you are not willing to spent that kind of
money for something used, beware damaged or worn out. You are
not willing to buy garbage. You are also not willing to spent that
kind of money for something that is not entirely yours, something
that isn't virgnal, something that another guy already wore on his
wrist.

You know deep in your heart that every little scratch you find
on the case of any used watch you purchased will grow in your mind
to the size of an elephant and will spoil basically everything. You
would start to hate that watch for not being perfect, for wearing
marks of a former owner. And there is only one way to avoid this
worst case scenario: buy your first Rolex new.

Despite other voices on the internet that tell you that this is
your first big mistake I don't blame nobody for doing so. I myself
wasn't willing to buy my Sea-Dweller used. I didn't even consider
it. It was a watch that was available new, so why go for used?

Additionally I felt a very natural skepticism against all that
many gray market dealers that offered all kinds of watches: new
ones, used ones, vintage ones (basically worn out old watches that
look a bit busted for extremely serious money). Being a watch
novice, I did not feel confident that I would be able to distinguish

a good used one from a not so good used one. I, beware!, wasn't even confident that I would be able to tell a real one from a (well made) fake or even worse get a Frankenstein watch. No, Victor Frankenstein did not make watches, not even Rolex fake watches.

When you start out with luxury watches you basically normally don't know anything about watches. You don't know how a real Rolex feels on the wrist and in your hand, how it really looks, how it impresses your senses. So in this state you are prown to any fake dealer with a fake watch until you learned some. But you can only learn having one, so you are clearly in a starter kind of problem.

But the situation is worse than that. Indeed older Rolex models, those Rolex sold until about 2009 were all quite different from todays Rolexes. To someone who only knows the recent solid-bracelet-supercase-models, the older models until around 2009 seem so light in the hand and so different, however well made, that a lot of people indeed think they are fake Rolexes.

Figure 3.6: Rehaut imprint around the dial

And these older but still rather recent models often also don't have those, features Rolex solely introduced to make it harder for the fake-manufacturers to copy a Rolex watch in the first place: like the Laser-printed rehaut (the inner ring of the bezel around the dial, that today says ROLEX ROLEX ROLEX...), or the tiny Rolex cron on the crystal at 6 o'clock, you nearly cannot see with the naked eye. So people who hear about these features tend to think a Rolex that does not have these, must be a fake. But that is not the case, as Rolex introduced these things only in the last 10 years.

So the fear is great when you buy your first Rolex to get a fake one and not be able to identify that. The result would be: your money is down the drain and you only got some piece of junk.

The cure for that obviously is to get your first Rolex from a official 'Konzessionär', an official Rolex seller. These watches can be trusted to be 100% original and new. No doubt about that. So you probably do one thing: you buy your first Rolex new for the official retail price – or perhaps 10% off. Or perhaps 10% more, if you absolutely want one of those sought-for icons.

Doubt and Savety

What you often hear is that if you buy retail from an official Rolex dealer, you loose money and therefore should always buy used, because the price is better – and a used Rolex is every part as good as a new one.

Well, I doubt that theory. Firstly, used watches obviously do differ a lot. They are not the same, because their former owner (or even owners) most definitely treated them differently. One guy bought a Explorer II and really went into mountain climbing and that sort of stuff, crashing it into boulders, wearing it in the cold and in the rain and snow and so on. The next guy bought the same Explorer II and put it on every day to go to the office. The third guy might buy the Explorer II and put it into a bank vault as he hopes it will go up in price over time. You can be sure that these three watches will experience different kind of wear and will be completely different watches when being sold on the used marked. Yes Rolex watches are tough, but even Rolex cannot do magic. Physics still apply also to Rolex watches. Secondly, it is said that Rolex (steel sports) watches never go down in price but steadily up. But if that is the case, you can of course buy retail, because the price of the watch will rise and after some years will definitely be higher than the price you payed for it. The price of the used piece shouldn't be much lower than the retail price at all – in this theory. Thirdly, if the risk is to get a fake watch or even a Frankenstein watch, you will never see your money again, so it is definitely better to get a new, original one from a official dealer than to have that sort of risk of loosing everything in the second of purchase.

Now, what is a Frankenstein watch? If you look at the Rolex watch market you find out that there is a lot of irrational love for some models, meaning, there are models that do not differ a lot from their siblings but are payed with seriously more money.

At the moment, the Rolex GMT Master II models are in such a situation. If you buy a used GMT 16710 from around 2007 you can pay $6000, $7000 or $8000, depending on the color of the bezel. If the bezel is black, red and black or red and blue makes a difference of 2000 bucks. The watches don't differ in anything else but the bezel. And since you can change the bezel rather easily, what do people do? They buy a black bezel watch, buy a red-blue bezel from the used market or from Rolex for $200 and put it on the watch. Voilat, you invested $6200 and can now sell the watch for $8000. If the watch has the 3186 movement instead of the 3185 (mark the huge difference!) you can add another $2000 to up to $10.000, if it is in NOS (new old stock) condition. There are also offerings for $30.000 (sic!) for these rather scarce models on the market. So you can try the same thing as with the bezel. You can remove the 3186 movement from a 16750 Explorer II, put it in a normal 3185 GMT Master II and you have the magical 3186-GMT and sell it for $20.000. So, often the dials in used watches are not original, or the hands. The older the watch is, the higher the risk that some guy took two watches and mangled them together into one wild piece trying to sell if for a premium price. All that is not exactly illegal, but of course highly unwanted as it spoils the whole watch. It puts together parts that were not meant by Rolex to be in one watch. But that still is not Frankenstein, it is just disgusting. And of course these pieces are not of that high value they are being sold for.

There are even less acceptable variations of that kind of piecing up and putting together on the market. There have been real Frankenstein watches spotted on the market that have original Rolex cases and bracelets, but cheap copycat movements inside. As not one Rolex has a display caseback and expecially the divers are sealed tightly you normally do not take the caseback off and look inside if there is a true Rolex movement inside. So you might use such a horrible 'thing' for some time until you find out that the precision of the movement doesn't seem to be what you expect from a Rolex. Then you take it to a dealer and... game over.

All this comes to mind when you ask yourself if you, as a novice to watches, are really willing to invest several thousand Dollars in a watch you cannot check if it is original at all.

That is why I went to a official dealer, payed (nearly) the retail price but are very happy and completely save from fraud with these watches. I just wouldn't take any risk with my new 8000 bucks watch.

So for the first (and at stage you often think: one-and-only) luxury watch I simply went the save way: I bought from an official concessionary Rolex dealer, there is nothing more official and save.

So I called the next dealer and asked if it was in stock... and... it was! What a surprise with a Rolex sports model!

Owning it, Wearing it

My choise was all too well. The Sea-Dweller is a marvelous watch. It gives you the confidence that you won't be able to even scratch it a bit. It is rock solid. The ceramic bezel and the sapphire crystal of course, but also the steel case and the brillant all new Oyster bracelet with the unbelievably rugged all new milled out clasp gives you the feel of a tank, a bank vault, something nearly indestructable.

Of course that is not true. As with all of these watches, it is nearly impossible not to scratch the clasp. After some time wearing

Figure 3.7: so cool: Rolex Sea-Dweller 4000 Ref. 116600 (2015)

it, despite that said above, you feel like it will scratch when you move it across some silk. Obviously the truth is somewhere in between.

To be honest, I know no better tool for timing cooking than the diving bezel of the Sea Dweller. I confess using it nearly all day as something like a Kitchen Dweller. You can use the bezel easily to time short intervals of up to an hour. That is quite perfect for cooking as most timing tasks are within that span.

Speaking of the bezel. The bezel mechanics of the Sea Dweller are just marvellous. Something you show to your wife saying: look here, now turn it, turn it,... do you hear that, can you feel it... isn't that great! Rotating it reminds you of selecting the right code on a safe from the last century. It is infinitely prezise and perfectly elegant. Compared to the fine clicks you sense with your fingertips and hear with your ears, the diving bezel of the Seamaster e.g. feels like a tin toy with just a fake function. The only bezel that comes close to that of the Sea Dweller 4000 I know, is the totally different, but likewise brillant bezel of the Rolex Yacht Master. Totally different, because this feels more like it was perfectly mounted on some kind of space technology ball bearings, withstanding some magic springs.

Wearing the Sea-Dweller 4000, it somehow became my smaller, easier to wear Deep-Sea. As cool as the big one, but wearable all day. The Deep-Sea is a undoubtedly a holy grail watch. It is so merciless, so brutal, so over the top, that it just *has to* become a classic, or even still is one. It's like, let's say, the Lamborghini Diablo: unusable, but very cool and for that reason even more exclusive than because of its pricetag itself. Because there are not only the people who cannot afford it, there are also those who don't want to be killed by their car and for that reason don't buy one. Well, you won't be killed by a Deep-Sea, but you perhaps are not willing to wear such a large and heavy fellow. And in sum the result is the same: exclusivity.

But the Deep Sea also can be found a lot on the used market – even the special James Cameron version with the beautiful blue dial. Why? Obviously that is the case *although* it is very cool, but *because* it wears immense, almost unwearable – at least, if you don't have wrists like Arnold Schwarzenegger.

The Sea-Dweller 4000 is also rather big. Especially everytime I wore the 36 mil Explorer 1 (see below) for some days – what I often do and I do it full of joy – even the 40 mil Sea-Dweller 4000 wears like the Deep-Sea itself. Everytime I have that experience I don't even want to find out how the real Deep-Sea would wear on my wrist after the very light, very small and very elegant Ex.

But that impression wears off quickly and the SD4 becomes what it truly is: a brillant and very cool watch and a great and very rugged daily wearer.

And not only that. As it has that indestructible feel to it, with it's indestructible ceramic bezel, with it's indestructible saphire crystal, with it's not indestructible but very very solid bracelet and clasp, it makes a great adventurer's watch. So I took it to the mountains to see what's what...

And because of its utter ruggedness, the Sea-Dweller makes a brillant daily wearer. It not only feels, it literally *is* so tough, that you probably loose a finger or crush a bone before you can damage the sapphire crystal or the ceramic bezel.

Figure 3.8: inappropriate for the species: Rolex Sea-Dweller 4k on a mountain

And one word about the superluninova. At first I was disappointed. Even though I read everywhere that it shone so bright that you litterally could use it as a torchlight (which in the true sense of the word is of course bogus) I could not find it shining very bright nor very long. So I put it into direct sunlight for some minutes, put it on my arm and... same thing: after some 1 to 2 hours the visibility wore off to just not visible at all. I was disappointed. And that got just a little better, when I got my brand new Panerai Luminor, which has the light litterally in its name, that basically showed the same phaenomenon.

And now I did, what more often than not helps: I chose to be patient (not my strong point usually). And that helped. Because now, after I wear the watch for a year and it regularly got exposed to sunlight, the superluminova works better and better. It sometimes is so bright that it amazes me.

Finally: the ups and downs

The only down I could find till now is that the Sea-Dweller 4000 is really a professional diving watch. That means, if you service it,

Figure 3.9: Desk-Diver: Sea-Dweller 4k on a Desk

all the water tight sealings cannot just be opened and closed again. It seams, that the 'seals' are more kind of glue, that tightens the case against 400 bars of pressure. They all have to be replaced everytime the watch is opened for service, what obviously will not be very cheap. So what you can hope is that the brillant Rolex 3135 movement inside the SD4 will not need a service for a very long time.

And no: the bezel is not indestructible and if you destroy it, things are getting really expensive. But who does? I estimate you have to use a hammer to damage this thing – at least it feels that rock solid.

Weaknesses

The Sea-Dweller in my eyes has only two weaknesses:

Firstly, it is a bit on the heavy side and a watch with less heft and stance wears a bit more comfortable. It is obviously meant to be a smaller Deep Sea and technologically it is. But with the new bracelet it is still a quite heavy watch.

Secondly, the date. Even if you prefer the Sea-Dweller because it has no cyclops lens over the date, the date sometimes... ok, make it 'often'... the date is often hard to read. Compared to my rather similar Omega Seamaster it is 'often' not readable at all. The fact that the dial is rather thick and black and the date is somewhat below and on a white plate does not improve things as the small numbers of the date are often partly in shadow. If you compare it to the Yacht-Master (see below) with the cyclops, you understand why Rolex uses the cyclops more often than people like it.

However my verdict is clear: Would I buy the Sea-Dweller again? Yes, any day of the week.

State of the Watch Collection

Now this is getting momentum. Although I still did not considered myself being a watch collector I already had a small collection of four interesting pieces and two not so brillant but very personal pieces with some emotional value for me.

Figure 3.10: A two-piece Collection

There now are some pocketwatches from the early 1900s, two of them with reasonable value, a gold (plated) dresswatch from the 1960s, a quartz dresswatch from the 1980s, an Omega Seamaster and now the Rolex Sea-Dweller 4000, a classic from the early 1970s in its latest incarnation with technology from the 2010s

Rolex models, milled out clasp, solid links bracelet, Supercase with
ceramic bezel and the Maxidial.

Two great pocketwatches, two not very exclusive dresswatches,
but two mechanical luxury divers both the the potential to become
absolute classics of the modern era. Something you can absolutely
built on.

Chapter 4

The Watch Industry

An overview over the related companies, brands and groups.

The hundreds of brands of the Swiss (and German) watch industry are quite boringly spread over not too many luxury groups who mainly came up during the 1970s and 1980s quartz-crisis that shook the Swiss (mechanical, non-quartz) industry to its very roots. Back then a lot of formerly independent manufacturers got in trouble or even out of business and only tight bundling of synergies like the Swatch Group or massive financial and entrepreneurial power like the Richemont Group made it for the manufacturers possible to survive to this very day.

Being part of a larger industry group has advantages and disadvantages. On one hand it opens up synergies and a strong financial backbone. On the other hand, the group management can force a company into using parts from the group because it is economically reasonable, however this does not mean that it is a good thing from a technological or aestetic standpoint. This can be the case in the Swatch group, where the interweaving of former independent and for that reason autonomous manufacturers are degraded to a mere brand that offers parts from the shelf (and not only from the top one). Of course brands like TAG Heuer or Longines come to mind in that context, former great watchmakers that offer average products nowadays. Others might benefit from the cooperation like Omega or Breguet, mainly because they are very strong brands with a uninterrupted tradition and due to their position on top of the heap get a lot of attention by the Group being some of their top sellers or top image representatives.

So if you buy a Omega or a Breguet or a Blancpain, be aware that you to some degree you always will get a watch from the Swatch Group in either way. Of course these highly traditional manufacturers also still have some degree of sovereignity, however due to efficiency it is not always transparent, where the know how, the perfectionism and the product focus of the manufacturer ends and the economic reasoning begins.

Swatch Group

The Swatch Group is organized and managed from Switzerland and thus is very aware of the mindset of Swiss culture and has a very stong connection to Swiss watch tradition. The key strategy is internal synergy and cooperation and a strong segmentation of the brands so that they do not compete but *complete* each other. From the top brand with the most tradition and heritage, Breguet, down to the most modern and radical Swatch brand every brand addresses a different market. The most important luxury watch brands that cooperate within the Swatch Group are (in bold print, who I consider important to the luxury watch segment, like we understand it here):

- **Breguet**

- **Omega**

- **Blancpain**

- **Eterna / ETA**

- Lemania

- Longines, Rado, Glashütte Original, Union Glashütte, Tissot

- Hamilton

- Swatch

Breguet   is an icon of watchmaking themselves. As early as 1780 Breguet invented the automatic watch, later the shock protection and the tourbillon. Breguet even made the first wristwatch in 1810 and of course they invented the Breguet-Hairspring. As early as 1795, Breguet had to mark their watches to fight illegal copies. When it comes to models they today lack a bit important and recognizable watches. Their watches are often quite complicated and real pieces of watchmaking art. But also a bit too much of everything and of course highly expensive. Their most renown icon today should be the Breguet Type XX, a pilot's chronograph.

Figure 4.1: Breguet icon: Type XX

Omega   Most of the watchmakers are lucky to have one eternal icon. Omega has two of them: the Seamaster and the Speedmaster.

Blancpain   of course managed to bring the first real diving watch of to the market with the Fifty Fathoms. The other two icons of diving watches, the Rolex Submariner and the Omega Seamaster were just late to the party. That makes Blancpain more or less one of those one-famous-model companies. Of course they do other watches, but their iconic moment in time clearly is the Fifty Fathoms – a serious diving watch to this very day.

ETA   is of course the centralized maker of movements for the big portion of the Swiss watch industry. Their watch brand 'Eterna'

Figure 4.2: Omega icons: Seamaster, Speedmaster and Speedmaster Mark II

Figure 4.3: Blancpain icon: Fifty Fathoms

is not widely renown, but as they for obvious reasons use 'inhouse' produced movements that have proven their quality and reliability in thousands and thousands of Swiss watches for decades, Eterna should be considered one of the major Swiss watch brands.

Lemania   is worth noticing because they used to make outstanding movements for several iconic watches. The most prominent is of course the Omega Speedmaster Professional, the Moonwatch.

Richemont Group

The Richemont Group is somehow the opposite to the Swatch Group. In short: it is not managed in Switzerland but in France, it is not mainly synergetic and cooperative but competitive. All watch brands and manufacturers within the Group basically try to be the best, to be top notch of the one luxury watch market, what somehow keeps them strong and independent as brands, but also weakens them due to the massive inhouse made competition and the sacrifice of synergy. The most important luxury watch brands that compete within the Richemont Group are (in bold print, who I consider important to the luxury watch segment, like we understand it here):

- **Vacheron Constantin**

- **Jaeger-LeCoultre**

- **A.Lange**

- **IWC**

- **Cartier**

- **Panerai**

- Piaget

- Baume & Mercier

As you can see, Richemont even has a Holy Trinity member (Vacheron Constantin) on its list. But it is hard to see, if that improves or weakens the standing of VC, because especially in the Holy Trinity and High Horology market, independence and maximized inhouse control of all parts and materials is considered important. In that sense the Richmont strategy of having not too much synergy between the manufacturers of the Group, by not mixing the heritage and technology of the memebers too much, seems to be the right strategy to not dilute the character and the standing of the brand. However, compared to the real 'independent' manufacturers like Patek, AP and Rolex, only being a member of a Group already weakens the brand massively.

We can also see that Richemont has 1 Holy Trinity member (VC), 2 High Horology manufacturers (JLC, A. Lange), 2 Luxury (IWC, Cartier) and 1 enfant terrible (Panerai). This seems quite well balanced and the immense Swatch Group has compared to that only 1 High Horology (Breguet), 1 Luxury manufacturer (Omega), 1 luxury brand (Blancpain) and a lot of non important brands that are basically powered by ETA movements and technology. So in terms of real luxury standing, Richemont outmanoeuvers Swatch a bit.

Vacheron Constantin   is of course one of the most important and respected watchmakers of the world. It is famous for being in business since 1755, uninterruptedly. But as very traditionalistic companies often do, VC is not known for its pure dynamic. Time, tradition, merits, success and reputation seems to make companies a bit stiff.

Figure 4.4: Vacheron Constantin icons: Patrimony and Overseas Chronograph

So today, they do not have outstanding models that drive their business a lot. There is of course the sporty Overseas. But this might also be the cause for the lack of VCs dynamic: today every watch is a dress watch. And traditional dress watch manufacturers have a hard time to compete agains those dramatic and provoking designs of the sports watches. And this seems to be especially true for VC.

Jaeger-LeCoultre is widely known for the outstanding, extravagant and elegant Reverso.

Figure 4.5: Jaeger-LeCoultre icons: Reverso, Master Control, Master Compressor

But even if the Reverso is their flagship, JLC makes a lot of very fine watches with brillant movements and a very stylish and timeless design language, like the Master Compressor dive watches and the Master Control dress watches. Jaeger-LeCoultre started out as the watchmakers watchmaker, as a company that supplied movements to a lot of other watchmakers, like even Patek-Philippe. And still today the US Navy Seals, where a watch can make the difference of life and death, ended up with a special version of the JLC Master Compressor GMT Chronograph. JLC is obviously the most underrated watchmaker in the whole lineup and would deserve much more recognition on the market than they actually get.

A. Lange is perhaps the best watchmaker in the world. But it has a probelm: it is not located in Switzerland but in Saxonia/Germany, right next to the Bohemian border.

Figure 4.6: A. Lange icons: Lange 1, Datograph, Zeitwerk

So it is only considered 'another' brillant watchmaker, but not for what it actually is: a class of its own, perhaps even above the Holy Trinity. The Lange 1, the Datograph Chonograph as well as the 'Zeitwerk' are outstanding masterpieces of watchmaking – and so are their prices.

IWC   makes heavy time measurement machines, not exactly watches. Ok... of course they make watches. But these are very application driven, often hugely oversized and meant for the serious user, not so much for the millionair who wants to toy around with some $10,000 watches. Their retro oriented Big Pilot watches (esp. the Ref. 5002) and the Portugieser lineup of elegant chronographs have inhouse movements and get significant reception.

Cartier   makes kind of very old watches. Their icons date back to the very beginning of the wristwatch era and even took a major part in starting it at all – and this was closely related to the 1st World War and the beginning of flight.

In the war, men needed a watch in direct access. Wristwatches up to that time were for women only, as they lacked the pockets to put pocketwatches in. But in battle as well as in a plane cockpit you had no time to fiddle about to find out the time. So Cartier was asked to make wristwatches for that application: flight. And out came the 'Santos' in 1904 and later in 1917 the 'Tank'.

Figure 4.7: IWC icons: Big Pilot (46 mm), Portugieser

Figure 4.8: Cartier icons: Santos, Tank

Panerai is merely an empty brand name with some heritage that Richemont akquired. The designs are inspired by originally oversized Rolex diving watch designs, Rolex shipped to Italy during the 1930s and 1940s.

The brutal, oversited military design of their icons, mainly the Panerai Luminor Marina and the Panerai Submersible had been a huge success in Hollywood during the 1990s and 2000s.

Figure 4.9: Panerai icons: Radiomir, Luminor Marina and Submersible

LVMH - Louis Vitton

Then there is the rest. Louis Vitton, a mere luxury and fashion brand from Paris has Hublot and Zenith and what is left of the former great Heuer manufacturer.

- **Hublot**

- **Tag Heuer**

- Zenith

- Bulgari

Hublot   is of course the newcomer and enfant terrible of the watch industry and was primarily a marketing monster what made them meanwhile a very strong brand. It is famous for its oversited Big Bang and Big Bang Unico models. Hublot is fun and entertainment, and famous for their courageous and colorful designs like the Big Bang Unico Usain Bolt.

TAG Heuer   has a great heritage and they try to connect to it with their vintage inspired models. These are mainly models from the 1970s when TAG Heuer, was only 'Heuer' and made original watches.

Figure 4.10: Hublot icons: Big Bang, Big Bang Unico, BB Edition Usain Bold

Figure 4.11: Heuer icons: Monaco, Monza, Carrera

Nevertheless it is still a well-known and strong brand and for that reason is mentioned here in some detail. The classics are all related to motorsports. The names of famous racing courses like Monaco and Monza shows that as well as the Carrera racing event. Especially the Monaco is considered as one of the design classics – even if I don't like it so much.

Zenith basically got famous because they could not ship as many El Primero chronograph movements to Rolex as they needed for their new Daytona in the early 1990s. This according to the lore caused the scarcity of that particular Daytona model (Ref. 11620) and is until this very day for that reason responsible for

the maketing gag that there are waiting lists of up to 10 years (!)
to get a new Daytona.

Kering Group

The importance of the merely 2 luxury watch brands of the Kering Group is quite uncertain.

- Girard-Perregaux

- Ulysse Nardin

And then there are the really small groups resp. independent watchmakers. And these read like the who-is-who of the real important brands:

Rolex Group (independent)

The Rolex Group is of course not a international corporation but consists only of the Rolex brand themselves and its sibling Tudor. Nevertheless they make 25% of all the money that is made in the watch industry worldwide. So strong is the Rolex brand name and its products.

- **Rolex**

- Tudor

Figure 4.12: Rolex icons: Submariner, GMT Master II and Daytona

Rolex is of course the maker of a lot of cult watches like the Submariner, the GMT Master and the Cosmograph 'Daytona'.

You can of course write a whole book about Rolex and the icons and models they have – why I of course have and you can of course find and read it in any major ebook store as well as as a paperback book.

Tudor is always the little brother of Rolex. Even if they managed to emancipate themselves by making not only older Rolex models but their own designs with their own movements, the brand still suffers from the heritage of being the 'poor man's' Rolex.

Breitling (independent)

Breitling is another military grade pilot's watch manufacturer – and here the name is program ('breit' is german for 'broad').

Figure 4.13: Breitling icons: Navitimer, Chronomat

Their icons are the hugely oversized pilot's watches 'Navitimer' from the 1960s and the 'Chronomat', its successor in spirit from the 1980s. Today Breitling watches are considered extremely robust, they make several inhouse movements and all of their watches have the COSC chronometer certificate. However not everybody likes the highly polished cases and bracelets that are really everything but decent. Breitling is together with Rolex and Omega the inner core of the luxury watch segment.

Patek-Philippe (independent)

Patek-Philippe has invented nothing less than the crown back in the 18-somthings – before that you needed a key to wind a (pocket-)watch. And they make outstanding movements.

Figure 4.14: Patek Philippe icons: Calatrava, Nautilus, Annual Calender

However they suffer a bit from the same illness that Vacheron Constantin has: they are at the top. Beyond that they define the 'dresswatch' to this day with the perfectly reduced Calatrava, they define what elegance and sportyness at the same time can look like with the Nautilus and finally they define what complications are with the Annual Calender.

Audemars-Piguet (independent)

AP today *is* the Royal Oak. Even if this might not completely do justice to a Holy Trinity manufacturer with a heritage dating back to the 1870s, it is more or less the case.

Although they make other watches, the whole brand is recognized for that revolutionary design from the 1970s, with its today's incarnations of the Royal Oak, the Royal Oak Chronograph and the Royal Oak Offshore.

In my opinion, it could be argued that AP is today number one in the watch industry. Although still Patek is considered the top manufacturer of the top manufacturers (i.e. within the holy

Figure 4.15: AP icons: Royal Oak, Royal Oak Chronograph and Royal Oak Offshore

trinity), somehow AP managed to be de facto number one.

The smuggled their watches onto all the wrists of alle the true aristocrats and celebrities. They today and for some time now, basically since the 1970 increasingly wear AP, not Patek. AP managed to make modern sports watches with the classic Royal Oak design as well as the more modern and hulky Royal Oak Offshore. And that way, they bascially don't produce holy trinity watches from the last century, like PP and VC still do, but make modern holy trinity watches that arrived right here and now in the 21st century. And that position, that ability to move with the market and at the same time be themselves and recogniced as such, makes them number One from my point of view. Sorry Patek, you are still great!

Now, this had been a lot of great watchmakers and some very nice watches. However, if you collect not only for fun and in hunt for beauty, keep in mind, that the brands that keep their value over time are scarce. It's basically Rolex, Patek and some Omega models.

Chapter 5

The Fake

Of course I wanted a Hublot. But I wasn't so sure if it was a good investment. For an ETA based cool design case from unconventional materials and with a size unclear if still fashionable in another 5 or 10 years, in short: more a hip fasion piece than an eternal piece of luxury, I was not willing to pay the hipster pricetag of 12.000 bucks. For 3000 or 5000 it would have been reasonable, because the fancy design would find its lovers even if smaller watches would be again en vogute, but 12.000! No way.

But I still wanted one.

The Original Design

Beyond the original Big Bang design, there is another heritage the Big Bang cannot deniy: Yes the Hublot Big Bang is a AP (Audemars-Piguet) Royal Oak (RO) clone and yes it is somehow cooler than the RO even the Offshore, because it is more modern and stylish, while the RO carries heavy on its pedigree and heritage. And the Hublot designers obviously are just a bit cooler than a lot of their collegues. The Big Bang somehow looks and feels a bit like the lightweight and light-footed version of a RO Offshore.

But on the other hand, with the RO you buy a Holy Trinity product, the best of the best of Swiss watchmaking, while with the Big Bang you get a cool designed case on a rubber strap with a all

Figure 5.1: inspired by: AP Royal Oak Offshore vs. Hublot Big Bang

too standard ETA movement in it. That is quite a difference!

You can of course argue that the Hublot Big Bang is just a cheap rip off of the Royal Oak Offshore with at an rather oversized price tag.

What matters is that you will find this distinction again in the resale value of both pieces when you check the value of your watches in some five or ten years. The RO will be high up and the Hublot will perhaps find afficionados for their design, but not very much more. That way your 12 grand will probably be, depending a bit where oversized sports watches will be still fashionable then, gone. This is way more probable than loosing your 20 grand with the Royal Oak.

Therefore Hublot tries to offer their latest Big Bang models with an inhouse (called Unico) movement. But as I said: not the fact that a watch features an inhouse movement makes it more valuable, but the extremely increased quality of the movement usually only feasible with complete inhouse control of all materials and parts. So perhaps this inhouse movements trend at Hublot, Breitling, Panerai and others is not very much more than a marketing gag. It only begins to make sense when these inhouse movements show a significantly higher quality than the usual ETA sourced movements they used before.

But I had personal doubts either: I was quite unsure if that immense design case would fit my arm – or if it would be just way too large.

So I decided to put my whole Hublot-affinity to the test and got a fake watch for that reason.

Considering the purchase

If you look for fake watches on the internet you will find a lot. Nearly every real luxury watch finds its copycat watch. But there are even more versions, as some of these watches have simple quartz movements and some have the exact copy of an ETA movement made in China.

This is all a big criminal mafia. I only considered for my test a cheap quartz version, as I never would have mixed up such a piece of junk with a real Swiss watch. It just isn't and it isn't still, even if it has a mechanical ETA copy in it. That just makes the whole thing even more criminal.

I wrote a lot about that fake watch stuff in Luxury Watches – a purchasing guide. I am not willing to repeat that here, because I am completely done with that. Fake watches are money down the drain. And that's it.

Fake Design

In the case of the dial options I decided for the real classic Big Bang design language with the huge numerical hour markers. And at first (knowing it being a toy that never would be part of my serious watch collection) the rose-gold design attracted me. But then my wife said, she would go for the steel version as the rose-gold version is a bit obnoxious. And I agreed reluctantly, but she was right.

Before I finally ordered the watch I read a lot of crazy stories on the internet like, how attorneys and customs officers would approach me and basically put me in jail. All of that of course didn't happen. Basically because I did not sell these, but was just

Figure 5.2: rose-gold or steel: Hublot Big Bang

the idiot who gives his money for utter junk.

Owning it, Wearing it

When I got the watch I was at first surprised about the quality. It was not, as I was afraid, completely unwearable, but an ok watch like you get for the same money from all the mid range fashion labels like e.g. Fossil or Esprit.

But owning that fake taught me a lot. First and foremost it taught me, that wearing a fake, you feel like being a fake yourself. And that is terrible!

Better be true and buy a Citizen or Seiko quartz and feel ok, than buy a fake, because it does not make you feel special, what a real luxury watch does, but cheap and lousy. It doesn't make you feel proud. It makes you feel that you pretend to be more than you really are. You just know that, it's there and that takes all the fun away.

A real luxury watch does the opposite: it makes you feel that there is more to you than meets the eye, it makes you feel precious, it makes you feel great.

It depends on what you expect from a watch. But as you won't be interested in luxury watches if you are just looking for something that tells you time, you probably at least fancy the cool and sometimes extravagant design and style of those high end timepieces.

And if that is all you expect from a watch, being some cool looking piece of shit, you are most probably not a watch aficionado but just some guy who is looking for the next fashion piece.

Then of course you will never buy a luxury watch because you do and always will consider them way too expensive.

If you are unsusceptible to the fascination of a true luxury piece that really deserves the price of some thousand Dollars, you will never appreciate a true luxury piece.

And that is not me. I really enjoy the quality, the feel, the looks, the aura, the presence of a real luxury piece.

So I only wear the fake sporadically at best. More in the summertime at some outside events, never in the winter. Sometimes I put it on in harsh situations when I don't want to damage my really expensive, nice and beloved original watches, e.g. riding the bike in the countryside. So the fake Hublot does not get very much wrist time. I purchased it to wear it in situations when I did not want to wear my expensive watches, like, on a beach vacation, in dangerous sporty situations, or when I just wanted to test the Hublot form factor.

But all that did not quite work. Basically because the watch itself gives me the feeling of being fake, a liar, something that I am not, it isn't so much fun wearing it. When I wear it, I instinctively want to cover it up, not showing it to anyone, like it being a shame and I catched me at saying to someone asking me for that watch 'this is only a fake' before anything else.

However it looks quite good on the wrist. But it of course doesn't live up to a real luxury piece in every detail, not in the surfaces, not in the ruggedness (e.g. the crown and the pushers that are rather flimsy), not in the precision of the manufacturing, obviously not in the materials themselves.

So it basically looks better from far, for other people, than it does for yourself, as you always see it very close. And that takes all the fun away, as you first and foremost and probably 'only' purchase and wear a luxury watch for yourself.

To be completely honest: it is just a piece of junk that looks a bit like a Hublot Big Bang. And for this 180 bucks is way too much money, even 20 bucks would be too much.

The bottom line is that I spent 180 bucks for that watch with no value whatsoever and as it is illegal to sell it, the money is completely down the drain instantly.

For comparison: I payed 2500 DM for my Seamaster in 1999 and would get roughly 2000 bucks for it today. Considering the currency change from DM to Euro with 2:1 and (realistic) inflation in the meantime I roughly did not loose a buck in 15 years.

The Hublot Design

However, the fake Hublot does one thing: it is kind of a marketing piece for the real one, it is a teaser product, a preview, a way to find out how the real one would be and wear.

You can wear the fake and you will find out: ok, I don't want a fake watch, because it makes me feel fake. But the Hublot design on the wrist is quite cool. It wears smaller than its dimensions sound like, the materials are quite comfortable, even light, and if you imagine them being made with a real luxury watch precision, quality surfaces and a 'real' mechanical movement, this thing would probably be gorgeous.

Also, readability of the large black dial with the large hands is brillant. You recognize immediately and intuitively what time it is. And you cannot say that of every watch out there. Especially not for some really expensive ones made from fancy materials.

So, my theory that the fake Hublot was something like a marketing tool for the real one turns out to be true everytime I wear it.

A Verdict

And as the way you feel is exactly what you will experience and ultimatle be in your life, I cannot recommend that move buying a fake watch and then feeling like a worthless fake yourself. It's

Figure 5.3: good design, bad watch: Hublot Big Bang Fake

not only bad for Hublot, because they loose exclusivity with every fake Hublot that is around (and exclusivity is the most important currency in luxury) and also bad for all the others, because in general luxury is diminished when everyone has such a (fake) watch on the wrist. It is especially bad for you, because a watch is a very personal thing, it connects to you, impacts you and if the impact is 'fake' you become 'fake' yourself!

On that rare occations, when I have it on the wrist, I usually recognize the following: the Hublot Big Bang design is cool, really cool. When J.C. Biver says, the Apple Watch looks like it was designed by a design student in the first semester, he somehow knows, what he is talking about. The Big Bang, his baby, is one of a completely different kind. The Big Bang is so individual, so cool, so groundbreaking elegant and at the same time sporty, luxurious and provoking, it is a truly great design.

Even in this unauthentic, clearly less refined version with the cheap plastic and cheap tin case and the even cheaper quartz movement inside, the design is beautiful to look at and a cool and sporty accessory at the same time. If this justifies the price of a real one ($12000 retail, $7500 used) is another chapter as it

basically is an ETA movement with a fancy case on a rubber strap –
Omega (not a cheap brand either) used to sell that kind of watches
like the Seamaster Professional for $2000. Quite a difference that
is, as Yoda would tell you. But it is very very cool.

With all that in mind: would I

a) buy another fake? No.

b) buy a real Big Bang? No, well I think I wouldn't either.
Perhaps... I am thinking about the newer version with the Unico
inhouse movement.

At the moment I would go for the real one, the classic one, the
Audemars-Piguet Royal Oak or the RO Offshore. The Hublot is
cool, but it is basically a fashion watch and for that it is ridiculously
priced. The Royal Oak is about 5000 bucks more but worth every
penny.

Chapter 6

The Italian connection

There is a litteral connection between Panerai and Rolex. Today we would complain about product piracy. But back then in the 1930s... Italy wasn't exactly the China of the time, but sort of.

In the 1920s Rolex introduced the first waterproof watch and a lady from England tried to swim across the channel wearing it, which was of course a big marketing hit for Rolex.

Later in the early 1930, Rolex developed a diving watch with a, at that time, immense case diameter of 47 mm. But the watch didn't make it to the market and Rolex soon stopped its development completely. Later after the war they gave that idea another try and presented the Submariner...

About the same time, when Rolex dropped the diving watch project, a small company from Florence, Italy, who made nautical instruments for the Italian army for decades, suddenly presented their first diving watch: a diving watch with an immense case diameter of 47 mm fitted with a Rolex pocket watch movement, they sourced from Switzerland.

So in my book, there is a litteral connection there. Panerai had close bonds with Rolex and the Panerai store in 'Firenze' proudly featured a sign that said: 'Swiss Watches'. Perhaps some Panerai official caught wind of the development and decided to do something similar... so far the lore.

The Deeper Secrets

Everybody says that the Rolex Submariner (at that time basically a Explorer with a rotating bezel), the Omega Seamaster and first and foremost the Blancpain Fifty Fathoms are the first diving watches, all released in the early 1950s when scuba diving was invented.

However, everybody also knows that Rolex already in the 1930s worked on a diving watch which somehow (in dark and not too good documented and a little bit silenced ways) mutated into the Panerai Radiomir featuring a rugged Rolex pocketwatch movement. So now: which one is the first proper diver? The Rolex Submariner or the Panerai Radiomir?

So, if you add one and one, none of these first mentioned divers actually were the first real diving watches as the Panerai already in the 1930s and later during the war supplied their Radiomir watches to Italian navy divers. It lateron mutated to the Panerai Luminor from about 1946 onward. And there is more.

This is definitely more than just a rumor. Panerai in Florence, Italy built Rolex movements into their watches. This alone is astonishing. But as it seems, Rolex also shipped the case, the water proof Radiomir case.

And it also can be shown that the 47 mm Radiomir case with the large Rolex pocketwatch movement was indeed a Rolex *development*. A Rolex catalog from the mid 1930s clearly shows a new Rolex model, a 47 mm diving watch, which is not similar to the Radiomir, it clearly *is* the Radiomir case.

So, Rolex developped, designed, made and shipped the case and the movement of the Radiomir. Basically there is a word for that: the old original Radiomir indeed *is* a Rolex. Somehow a lost-son kind of Rolex.

But why do they not talk about that, why indeed are they covering that up? Why is the Radiomir not today considered one of the most important watches in Rolex history and being the first proper diving watch even in watch history? It preceeded the Sub, it worked quite well, was used in the war... oh.

Think about it: first of all the Switzerland based Rolex obviously wanted their share of the war business, but did not at all want to be known for it. They wanted to make the buck but keep their shirt clean. Military supply is always a bloody business, so you can understand why Rolex did not publish a lot about that.

But this thing is not only about military supply alone. There is even more than that! Don't forget that, despite all modern hipness and coolness of the Panerai brand, the italian Navy did not fight in the war on the side of the american-british winners. They fought with and not against Germany. The Italians belonged to the coalition of fascist countries together with Germany, Austria, Japan, Turky and Hungary that lost the war and with that a lot of rights that free people in the world rightly expect to have. Fascist Italy even invented fascism, the word is derived from the italian word 'fasci' what means 'branch', meaning the distinctive mark the 'fascisti' used on their cloths to know each other in the beginning of their political movement.

Rolex did not make no mistakes in their history, they obviously just covered them up properly. Because here they interpreted Swiss neutrality to supply every party of the war with military equipment. Not of the highest moral standards to say the least.

So it obviously is not true that Rolex developed this first proper diving watch and dropped it because they did not trust the 47 mm case to be marketable. The truth seems to be that Rolex supplied the later loosing party of the war (the Italians in that case) with military equipment. They designed, developed, made and shipped the Radiomir watches – they only did not make that public (what is always suggested in case of military equipment) and lateron they found out that this was a good decision, because they supplied the looser of the war and with that the later so called war-criminals.

So the Sub became the first, the iconic, the one-and-only Rolex diving watch of all time. Just because the Radiomir and its customer was not quite so good for the Rolex image after the war.

Then the radioactive material Radium in the 'Radiomir' was replaced by 'Luminor' and so also the name of the watch changed and the crown was guarded by a patented construction and ready was the Panerai Luminor series.

Some more Details

As you can find out the cryptic name Panerai Luminor Marina means the following: first, Luminor is the name of the model line that says something about the form of the case. The Luminor case has 44 mm, a simple polished steel bezel and the Panerai patented characteristical crown guard that makes it very easy to unlock the crown moving just one lever, to wind the watch and with the same lever lock the crown again to gain full 300 m (30 bar pressure) water tightness.

Furthermore the Luminor models (lumen = light) derive their name from the luminescent material that stores sunlight and radiates it slowly illuminating the dial in darker moments. Before there was 'luminor' the older models in the Panerai model line are the Radiomir series, which resemble the historically older Panerai models from the 1930.

There are Luminor models with two different dials. The 'sausage' dials, so called because the luminescent material is printed onto the dial (looking a bit like sausages). The second type of dial is also a Panerai heritage kinda thing: here the hour markers and the numbers 12, 3 and 6 are cut out from the dial so the luminescent material below shines right through. Because of that structure these dials are called 'sandwich' dial. But to be honest: the different dials look very similar in reality, and only rather different on detailed high resolution photos of the dial.

Contemplating the Purchase

Depending on the movement the Luminor models are a little different in height. The PAM111 only has the hand wound ETA 6497/2 movement with 56 hours power reserve, called the OP XI (Officine Panerai 11). The automatic movements are a bit thicker because of the rotor, and thus have a little thicker case.

The Marina version has the additional small seconds register at

Figure 6.1: tough decision: Panerai Luminor PAM112, PAM111 or PAM005

9 o'clock. The corresponding PAM112 is basically the same watch, but without the small seconds. It is said that it even has the exact same movement with the small seconds, but just doesn't use it – a kind of detail that I deeply dislike, being completely non-technical and illogical.

In my opinion, it is essential for a hand wound diving watch (on which your life might depend) that you can always tell if it is running or not. So a non-seconds version like the PAM112, which is aestetically very nice because of its very clean and reduced dial, is simply not what I understand a serious tool watch should be like. It should be usable in the first place. And for that it needs a seconds hand to see if it is running properly.

Also the COSC supports that idea. The PAM111 has the COSC certificate, because COSC is able to measure its precision, because it has the seconds hand. The PAM112 isn't.

Talking about dials. Panerai does not offer the perfect Panerai watch. If you want to cynical, you could argue that this is because that way they sell more watches. The perfect Panerai watch would be a PAM111 *with* the Officine Panerai logo. Unfortunately there is no such model. You only get the 'sausage' dial with the logo or the 'sandwich' dial without the logo. And the corresponding model with the logo is the PAM005.

On the other hand, the PAM005 has the small seconds but

neither the sandwich dial (but the sausage dial) and it has no transparent caseback. But, and this is a real huge *big* but, it has the 'op'-logo on the dial. And although this sounds like really a first world luxury problem, it is really a hard decision to drop the logo. Just because it is really cool. But the PAM005 has too many disadvantages. So I got the 111. For it has the sandwich dial and the small seconds...

Sometimes you eat the bear and sometimes...

But one thing is clear: In my opinion the PAM111 is the essence of Panerai, the quintessential model. It has everything Panerai stands for: The cool italian design language that is masculine and brutal, but also elegant and balanced. Machismo and elegance. The stenciled sandwich dial with the large amount of luminova below it, shining through. The classical black dial with the clear, down to earth large white hour markers and not very much else. It even has the brown leather strap that a lot of historic Panerai models from the 1940s and 1950s have. The patented crownguard with the easiest mechanism available on the planet to unlock and lock the crown again for water tightness. And the, in my opinion important, vintage style small second at 9 o'clock. Without that, the dial seems a bit empty, all too simple. The small second gives the dial a more tool watch aura and at the same time a more masculine stamce.

Owning it, Wearing it

The PAM111 comes with a leather strap like nearly all Panerai watches. The leather strap is part of Panerais iconic design language – although it is rather uncommon, not to say illogical for a diving watch to have a leather strap. But the historical Panerai had it and so has the modern hommage.

And that is a problem. If you of course intend to keep the watch forever and not only use it but consume it, you can wear the PAM on the leather strap and everything is ok. But if you see the expensive luxury watch also as a kind of investment that will at least keep its value also during high inflation phases of the

Figure 6.2: bello: Panerai Luminor Marina PAM111 (2015)

economy, selling it someday most remain a possible option. And as you must know, you get the best price for a full set, meaning the watch, the original straps (best unused), the box, the papers and all additions.

The good news is, that with Panerai this problem is not as big as with other watches, because Panerai is literally made to change the strap and change the style of the watch very easily. So you have two options to keep the original Panerai strap untouched and as good as new: you either buy a second market strap and wear that instead of the original one, or you use the rubber strap that is also part of the Panerai set. The rubber strap is much better and wears with much more comfort than you might expect. And after all: the PAM111 is a military watch for gods sake! Nobody tried to make it comfortable, it is supposed to save your life in combat. So if it wears a bit rough, this is just the character of a military watch. If you want a comfortable luxury watch and don't want to mess with straps, get a Rolex Explorer I 36 mm. This is comfortable and it fits under every cuff you'll ever wear.

All that don't-use-the-original-leather is of course a bit of a pity, because the original strap is, despite most of the fotos of it, very beautiful. The leather is soft and the color is darker than you can see in most of the pictures of the watch.

Panerai is famous for the versatility of their watches, especially the Luminor series as it can be used as a sports watch, as a military watch or even – with its shiny steel bezel – as a slightly oversized dress watch. The design of the watch is masculine enough for the first, brutal enough for the second and elegant enough for the third alternatve. What you indeed realize depends on what kind of strap you use. And that is why Panerai encourages you to swap straps a lot and for that reason there is a huge market of secondary straps especially for Panerai watches.

Figure 6.3: luminescent: Panerai Luminor Marina PAM111

To be honest I don't swap my Panerai straps very often. As I said I save the original leather strap to have a full set with an unused strap in vase I decide to sell it. And I indeed like the rubber strap, as with it the watch wears very masculine and military style.

Is it too large? Panerai is famous for its oversized watches. 44 mm, 48 mm. Not so much the rather old PAM111. First produced in 2002 it is more one of the Panerai classic and archetypical models. With 44 mm case diameter it is not an exceptionally small watch but with 15 mm it still has a decent height and with 136 gramms it is rather light, because it has no heavy bracelet but a rather light strap.

Overall, the case diameter to me seems overrated when you discuss wearablilty and comfort. The mass and the distribution of the mass, mainly here the height of the watch is more important than the case diameter. See the discussion of this fact down in the chapter Wrist-Time.

At the moment the PAM111 is becoming my favourite summer watch.

Lessons Learned

But one question remains: is it a original model? Or is it a fake? Is it a hommage? What is it? The question is: do you want something true, something original, or a sorrogate, a homage, a copy, however elaborated.

Let's see it that way: when it comes to historic 'vintage' models only the old original is the original. But they are often old, worn out, more for the museum than for the wrist, and small in numbers, not available at all, even dangerous to use (radioactive dials), and sometimes even ridiculously expensive. In historically important watches of course only the original is the original, but we have several stages of new watches that come near to it (or not so much).

So **stage 1** of originality would be an identical watch made ever since, the situation you also have with every new watch model. If you buy a new or used 116660 Rolex Deep Sea you get exactly that – and nothing that looks like it but in essence isn't.

Stage 2 would be something like the Speedy, basically the same watch with slight adjustments to optimize technical performance or ease of maufacturing.

So next to the original is the continuously made original model with none or very slight changes to it, like you find in the 1963 Omega Speedmaster Moonwatch. The only changes that have been made to this watch over the course of time are slight optimizations to the movement. The rest is still the same: same manufacturer, same case, same crystal, you get the idea.

The next **stage 3** is something like todays Rolex Submariner or the Patek Philippe Calatrava in reference to its classic predecessors: same original manufacturer, same model, same performance properties (or evolutionary better), same overall appearence, but evolution of all important features over time. Like a Porsche 911. Same basic idea, but improved in every single part.

Of course then here follows **stage 4**: watches that differ more and more from their famous predeccessors, but still are from the same manufacturer with the same technology pedigree. Like all modern watches from original manufacturers that have undergone massive changes and improvements to their appearence and technology, like todays Omega Seamaster Professional in reference to its predecessor, the Omega Seamaster 300 from the 1960s. The vast majority of all model lines from every manufacturer that is still a decent watchmaker belong in this club. The only reservation I see here is that the company itself should be more than just a brand name bought from some bankrupsy assets by some investor party.

Then there is **stage 5**: a watch that seems to be connected directly to some famous or important predecessor, but isn't. These are all the technologically not related but in design and appearence resembling their forefathers like the new James Bond Omega Seamaster 300. Looks like the original from the 1960s but in every detail isn't.

And with this special watch Omega also tries to do some very subtle but also very perfidious fake history, it's basically fraud: in the true history of that time, in the original movies of the 1960s James Bond always wore a Rolex Sub. The watch that Sean Connery used on set was a Sub. And now, Omega tries to alter that history by suggesting that there would be an Omega-James-Bond-vintage-historic-connection that they celebrate with the 'revived' 1960s Seamaster. This is devilish marketing. As there is no truth is such a historic connection whatsoever.

Also the reissues of historic Tag Heuer models e.g. like the Monaco or the Monza unfortunately belong here. They are just a shadow of themselves and one must doubt that there is much left from the glorious old days here other than the brand name.

Then follows **stage 6**, where the new Panerai models belong to: same principle idea, same recognizable design, but different manufacturer (who in case of Panerai obviously bought the rights to use the brand name and model names as well as all patents and transfered everything from Florence to Switzerland), different movements (at first ETA based then own inhouse, but no Rolex movements, what would be the only historically accurate version).

To be honest, this kind of watch is closer to a hommage, to a fake, than to the original. The only major difference is that these hommage watches are made with juristic and economic permission of the original rights owner. And of course that they are made with the orginal Swiss precision and perfectionism, not with the very bad quality of the 'real' Chinese fakes. The Tudor models of original Rolex models also belong here in this level of originality. I fear also other to Switzerland relocated brands like Hamilton belong in this category.

WTF?

Why is all that of any importance?

Because *heritage* is spelled in capital letters in horology. This is a very conservative business and the brands stongly emphasize the achievements their products had made in the past – even if it is a very long gone past.

It is basically a marketing strategy: if your products do not differ so much because of the lack of technological innovation and they cannot do so many different things (besides showing time and date and a bit more in that same range of things), you have to think how you can make your product more impressive than all the many others that do basically the same thing.

And heritage and past achievements is a reasonable way to do the trick, especially when the main innovations are in an area that is impossible to impress people with, like inside the movement and the use of innovative materials. This makes all too many people yawn, so you need something better, something much better. And if the product itself is very limited in the possibilities like cool design and cool functionality, you try to connect something very cool and attractive to your product and your brand. Like movie stars, movie characters, celebrities, top level achievers, like men on the Moon or on the Mount Everest or in the depth of the ocean's abyss.

That's why all this heritage thing is (made) so important in horology and all the models have the same names for decades. They try to keep the memory alive in the 2016 Rolex Explorer that Edmund Hillary back in the day had a Rolex on his wrist when he reached the peak of Mount Everest. And they try to sell today's Explorer with that memory. Not without success, one must admit.

So obviously something that is quite close to that watch on top of the Everest is somehow dearer to the watch buyer and collector than something that is farther away from it. And so everything must be closely connected and related – or at least pretend to be.

And this of course in a strange way contradicts the fact that a modern watch is much better than an old one. Even if you had an old watch from a time machine with no wear and no aging at all and would compare it to the modern one, you without a doubt would find the modern one better in many ways.

So a bit this whole heritage strategy fights back in form of the vintage watch movement, that basically holds old watches dearer than new ones. The fault is simple: if you constantly tell people of the great tradition and the great heritage and the achievements back in the 1960s and 1950s, people want the original (Level 1) watch from that era and not some more or less nice modern successor. Even if this, from a technological standpoint is in most cases total nonsense.

So when it comes to collecting watches that should keep their value, my simple idea would be, to buy either level 1 pieces in the form of new or nearly new used watches or buy level 2 (if there would be many pieces in that category) but stay away from the others as they are selling something to you that is not true at all. And over time only truth will stay.

In this train of thought it was a mistake to add the Panerai to my collection. But sometimes not only inner value counts but also long term fashion. And for that reason I still believe that if some demand and passion will be left of the Panerai craze of the last 20 years, it would be for one of the real classic models from that era, like the PAM111.

However...

In the sense of Level 6 the PAM111 is not exactly a hommage, but a watch in its own right, just because it is *different* from the old Panerai/Rolex watches from 1936 to 1956. It is a watch designed with this heritage in mind, but creating a watch in its own right, not just a copy of an old watch.

You of course cannot say that about a clear hommage like the PAM587 and even more about a fake-vintage design with a brownish fake-aged dial like the PAM662. And that is why I would never purchase one of them.

With a basic ETA movement the PAM111 on the other hand with just a small seconds 'complication' in a steel case it is a simple but honest watch. And one thing always counts: simplicity means durability and ruggedness. ETA movements power millions of Swiss watches. They are far from being a bad choice.

Summing it up...

So the bottom line is: there are no new 'real' Panerai watches. The last real Panerai Luminor models have been shipped to Italy by Rolex in 1959. And in that sense there are no 'real' vintage Panerai watches either as these are indeed Rolex watches with the Panerai label on them. Makes me wonder, what's there in it today?

So also my Panerai Luminor Marina is a hommage at best. But, to save its reputation, a high quality hommage from the original owner of the brand – well sort of, as the brand today is owned by Richemond, just like e.g. Cartier, Jaeger-LeCoultre, IWC Vacheron Constantin (!) and A. Lange (!!). And what's more, it is an hommage to a Rolex original design. So, did I make a mistake purchasing it?

It is a hommage to a extremely rare and for that reason extremely collectible Rolex (sic!) model that was shipped to Panerai in Italy from 1936 to 1956.

But that model was a real Rolex with a Rolex movement and a Rolex case. It indeed was the first Rolex professional diving watch design. And that makes it even more desirable as that ads a high historical and horological importance to the pure rareness.

But does this make it a collectible watch? No, probably not. But it is a cool design and for that reason it is a pleasure wearing it. And probably it becomes a collectible someday in its own right. Until then one can hope that it keeps its value somehow and that I have fun wearing it.

Purchasing a Panerai anyway

What you need to know when you think about purchasing a Panerai is that only the 1940 and 1950 cases are historically accurate. The 1993 designed cases like the Luminor and Radiomir of the 1990s and 2000s are more inspired by the original ones than very similar to them. So if you intent to purchase a rather historically accurate model, it had to be the 47 mm Radiomir 1940 case with a hand wound movement.

Figure 6.4: historically accurate: Panerai Radiomir 1940 models: PAM587, PAM662, PAM339 (source: Panerai.com)

Like e.g. the PAM662, PAM587 or the PAM339. And if

you tolerate a very practical automatic movement (despite the inaccuracy that the historical models had none) the PAM572 or PAM619.

Don't forget: the original Radiomir was a Rolex.

State of the Watch Collection

Not this collection gets into the second gear. An Omega, a Rolex and a Panerai steel diver.

Figure 6.5: Three Divers: A three piece Collection

Chapter 7

Yacht-Master

I first saw the Yacht Master with the platinum dial in italy worn by an elderly Brit in the pool. Now, if you meet Brits on vacation they often wear strange things at the pool: shorts and business shoes with socks for example. But this guy wore a Rolex Yacht Master in the pool playing with his grandchildren. That was kinda cool. But much cooler than that was the look of the watch itself.

Seeing it in the wild, I wanted to have the Yacht Master right away. What a beautiful watch glittering in the sun and with water around. The name Yacht Master was obviously the absolute right choice for that design.

After the cool black-on-black Sea-Dweller and the very no-nonsense military style Panerai I obviously needed some more bling in my life. Inspired by the unbelievable glittering looks, the Sea-Dweller has in sunlight with its white gold indexes glittering like stars in the sun, I knew a wanted more of that.

Purchasing it

Of course I purchased it retail, brand new. This time it was much easier than with the first one. I just called the dealer, if it was in stock, went there, put it on, thought about it for some minutes and bought it. Period.

Figure 7.1: Platinum glowing in the sun: Rolex Yacht Master

Owning it, Wearing it

One more advantage of Rolex watches: they almost always come on a bracelet. And that also helps keeping value. Think about it: if you wear a leather strap it inevitably wears off over time. This is different with a proper bracelet. And that adds to the long-term value of the piece, because you basically *can* wear a Rolex watch with a bracelet without damaging it at all – if you keep an eye on it a bit.

The Yachtmaster is not only a watch you can perfectly wear in a wet environment like the eponymous 'Yacht', but also in the winter.

It really has that iced look. Everything on it is clear and cold and like ice. Of course the 'iced' idea often refers to a watch that has been cluttered with diamonds over and over. But this is not only massively expensive it is also in my opinion ridiculous and lacks any style whatsoever. I basically hate that and in my opinion these changes destroy a watch – even more than e.g. coating it with a black titanium-nitride.

But the 'iced' look of the Yachtmaster is different. It is genuine. It is decent, it is classy, you just realize it on the second or third look. But it is true and so the Yachty is not only a summer-sun-yachting-fun watch but also a winter-ice-and-snow one.

The Yachty, despite being a comfortable luxury watch in the first place comes without the quick-adjust feature in the clasp of the Oyster bracelet. And that is not really understandable, it is indeed kind of non-sense, as a luxury piece should basically have all the comfort there is available – but if you have it, you find out that this doesn't matter at all.

This all depends on how you prefer to wear your watch. A watch on a bracelet can be worn in two basic ways: the hardcore military commando style, the watch being fixed on your wrist, the bracelet sitting tight on your arm, just the way you would wear a strap.

Or, on the other side, the bracelet loose, with more than 5 mm gap between the bracelet and your arm, relaxed, minding not if the watch moves around on your wrist a bit, slides down to your hand and up a bit your lower arm, when you move around. There is of course an extended version of that loose style that can only be used by women, with the watch being like a kind of heavy jewelry hanging, sliding and rotating on their lower arm.

I prefer the (manly) loose one. And for that reason, I do not necessarily need the fine adjusment function of the bracelet, in fact, it is better if I don't have it like with the Yacht Master, because that way I don't think about fine-adjusting the bracelet altogether.

I am not saying the fine adjustment feature of the newest Rolex clasps is a bad thing. It is a technically elegant solution, it is rugged and very useful if you prefer or need to wear your watch commando style. But if you don't, you don't need it that badly – and probably that's why Rolex decided to not offer it with the not-at-all commando style Yacht Master.

The whole purpose of a luxury watch is to make you feel even more precious. And that's why a precious metal luxury watch makes you feel even more precious than a steel one – and for that reason is better.

But there is a problem: the watch you wear should fit your overall appearance, your standing, your luxury factor, basically

Figure 7.2: hot and cold: Rolex Yacht Master Ref. 116622 (2015)

the content of your purse. It makes no sense to wear a yellow gold piece when your income is at best average. It does not fit. Everyone can see and feel the misfit. Everyone can see how you behave, what you think, if you belong to the kind of people you try to look like – or not. And if you don't, the yellow gold piece basically makes you look like a wanker. You are trying to look like way more than you in truth are.

The solution to that prob is: wear a precious metal watch (that is what you know) that is decent because it looks to the uncanny eye like a steel one (what is all the others need to know). Just be more than meets the eye, not less. Understatement is the best potion against looking like a wanker.

All that means: if you don't drive a Lambo, just go for white gold – or platinum version. And there we are at the classic Yachty Platinum and steel.

It's all about you and how you feel wearing it. It's never about others. That's why fakes don't work. That's why they indeed make you feel worse. The way a luxury watch makes you feel is not about how you are perceived by others. It's all about you and how you perceive yourself.

You shouldn't give too much attention to what people say. Of course the Yachtmaster isn't a Gay-Master as the Submariner isn't a waiter's watch and the many other insults the have-nots find to ease their envy.

Yes the Yachty, especially the Platinum version blinks and glitters like no other decent Rolex. The white gold hands and hour markers, the platinum bezel with white gold numbers and the polished case and bracelet centerlinks are just beautiful to behold – especially in the sun. It is definitely the definite watch for sailing on the oceans of the world – or any other lake big enough to put a boat on it. I for myself prefer a paddleboat because I don't have a sailboat or a yacht. I don't even have a motorboat. But that doesn't matter at all as this fun is all about being on the water, in the sun, in the wind, in my case in view of the alps in the distance, castles on the shore, beautiful and relaxed people all around, nature, beer, I admit, I am bavarian. And I love it!

And the Yachty is the ideal stunner for that environment to enjoy live on a summer Sunday in the beach lounge area with some relaxed easy listening music. Perfect fit.

Figure 7.3: in its element: Rolex Yacht Master

But keep in mind: Rolex not only makes you an addict, it also makes you a watch snob.

If you have one Rolex you will probably get a second (this) and a third one (read on). Not because the first one wouldn't fit your needs or what you expect from it but quite the opposite: it is so utterly brillant and makes you feel so special the you just want to repeat that experience (and then again and again and again...)

And from Rolex there is just one way: to the next Rolex or further up the hill to, lets say, Jaeger-LeCoultre, Audemars-Piguet, Patek Philippe, A. Lange, and those kind of guys. There is no way down. You won't sell yourself below price. The only exception might be watches with an overwhelming heritage, like the Omega Speedmaster Moonwatch – who can say, he was on the moon?

Family Ties

Of course the Yachty is a Sub. Kind of a luxury version, but essentially a Submariner. It has the water tight crown, the diving bezel, the 3135 movement, the cyclops lens and the Oyster bracelet and clasp. Even if it is obviously meant to be worn above sea level and not below, it is still waterproof to a degree that it can be understood as a full blown diving watch.

With its glittering platinum bezel, the Yachty one the arm somehow makes a similar impression like the Datejust with its classical fluted glittering whitegold bezel. But where the Datejust looks a bit old school and the large cyclops lens distorts its smallish 36 mil case crystal, the 40 mil Yachty has neither of these problems. It's just brillant and glittering and blinking like a star.

And it wears very very well. As it is kind of a precious metal Sub, with its platinum bezel and its platinum dial, it is closely related to other two-tone models, besides the awesome detail that this two-tone is a combination of silver gray steel and silver-gray platinum. The only two-tone I find acceptable. Even if you can clearly see the completely different matte shimmering tone of the Platinum surface. You see it. That's the whole point.

The reason why he Yachty wears so comfortable is the case. You feel it clearly everytime you put it on. It fits like a charm, caresses

Figure 7.4: theme and variation: the Submariner Family (Sub Nodate, Sub Date, Yacht-Master, Sea-Dweller, Deep Sea)

you arm more than sitting on it. No Yachty has the Supercase but the case form of the precious metal Sub and the Daytona with the elegant narrow horns that hold the bracelet. And that is good.

All great Rolex models, perhaps every great watch, every great piece of art and style all have one thing in common: decidedness, focus.

And so is the Platinum Yachtmaster. It makes no prisoners. You either like it or go to hell. There is no in between, no perhaps, no that's just like you opinion. Black or white. If you like it you'll never sell it. And I estimate that's the readon why there are nearly no used ones on the market. Because it's utterly brillant.

Value

You don't see the Yachty a lot. It's kind of scarce.

The watch market is a market, and so the value of a specific good is being recognized by every closed sale anew. But there is another value that is found differently: scarcity. If you look for used Yacht Masters on the market you will find that there are not so many.

That of course is due to the fact that a Yachty are not one of the entry priced volume models like the Subs, but there is also another factor in my opinion: if you have one, you don't want to sell it again, just because it is so great! It wears great, it looks great, it is rugged and practical. I hear everytime even people who might have bought it a bit skeptical find out that it makes even a perfect daily wearer (if you watch your step a bit).

Weaknesses

The weak point of the Yachtmaster is readability of the time – but not the date. Thanks to the cyclops this reads perfect and easy always.

The watch is clearly made for sunny days in bright daylight. There and then it reads quite perfectly and the dial shimmers like a trasure chest. But let there be less light, stormy clouds, indoor lighting, or, beware, twighlight, all you can see is a gray (beautiful) dial where must be something like hands that are supposed to show time – but actually don't.

It doesn't help that things get a little better again in darkness, as there you then again can see the luminescent hourmarkers and hands.

So the verdict here is:

Would I purchase the Yachtmaster again?

Yes, but not to find out what time it is. Just because it is an utterly beautiful piece that wears like a charm.

Oh no! There is a second weakness: the Yachty is a real precious metal two-tone watch, with a lot of platinum on and in it – what is basically cool in the first place! But, this platinum bezel is not as rugged as a ceramic one, by far not!, it is not even as rugged as the standard Submariner aluminum bezel.

And it is not only delicate but expensive too, as it is made from platinum (remember?). And it is not so easy to work with platinum as it is with steel or gold.

So when I bought the Yachty, the jeweler did not forget to tell me that they have an excellent watchmaker available who also is able to repair such a delicate and basically non-repairable thing as this platinum bezel. That makes you feel instantly confident.

State of the Collection

With the Yacht-Master, the Collection gets another diver, even if it is positioned as a above-the-waterline yachting watch. In some aspect it is a return to the style of the Seamaster, as the Yacht-Master does wear just as comfortable, light and precise as the formidable Seamaster Professional.

Figure 7.5: Four divers. But not the usual suspects, like the Submariner or Submariner date.

Chapter 8

The GMT Master

Buy now or cry later. This rule does not applie for a lot of watches, but for not so many more than for the last no-ceramic Rolex GMT Master II, the famous, the one and only: Ref. 16710.

In my watch collecting efforts, things had to become serious again. With this purchase I could no longer deny that I had become something I never imagined: a Rolex collector and a Rolex fan.

I always knew that I wanted the GMT Master II Pepsi. But it wasn't so easy to find out which one. When I entered 'GMT Master II' in Google or in Pinterest to check out the models I got rather different looking watches. Some looked old and strangely simple, although I could not exactly pinpoint what the exact differences were, some looked brutal and new and not very elegant and only some seemed to be the right ones I was looking for.

I had to learn that the GMT Master Pepsi was a watch that Rolex built since the 1950s. At that time PAN-AM pilots for the first time in history due to the development in intercontinental flight, changed many timezones so quickly that they should have a decent watch that was able to change the time very easy in hour steps back and forth – and Rolex made that watch for them. The GMT Master.

The iconic Pepsi bezel was there from the beginning, indicating night and day for the 24 hour hand. But the model got some changes over the decades. Slight changes, you probably only would spot if you know what you are looking for – we are talking about Rolex – but changes that make the models differ a bit.

But in 2007 Rolex changed the model dramatically with the step from Ref. 16710 to 116710. The new GMT got the Supercase, the Maxidial, the new Oyster bracelet with the polished centerlinks and of course the ceramic bezel with a new font for the 24-indexes. They changed everything. The whole banana.

I knew that I did not like the bigger fonts on the ceramic bezel. And I did not think that the Supercase was right for a more elegant sports watch like the GMT. Problem was: they were discontinued since 2007 and so I had to do what I never wanted: I had to purchase a used watch.

And I knew that I did not want a really *old* watch that, say, older than 10 years. So my choise was obvious: I wanted an Ref. 16710 from about 2005.

Purchasing something for more than 5.000 bucks from a official dealer is one thing. Buying a use thing from a not so official and authorized dealer is different. And looking for the one single watch from a whole range of differing watches, like ones from the early 2000s, others with other bezels, other bracelets, some with box and papers others without and so on, is not so easy.

You want to avoid getting something bad or even nothing at all.

Dial Variations

The GMT gets a lot of interest from the collectors in these days. Why? Just because the new model 116710 was changed in nearly every conceivable way. The old 16710, especially the Pepsi version is an icon and it became highly collectible as it is completely discontinued and there isn't even a new Pepsi version you could buy, as the only one available is in whitegold. So yes, you can buy it, but only if you are willing to spent 30 grand on it. Which I wasn't.

Stick Dial won't help you a bit and here is why: The different GMT dials, the stick dial, the rectangular dial and the, well, normal

Figure 8.1: Rolex GMT Master II Ref. 16710 (2004)

dial, are only correlated to some time of production. Nothing more. And that is fine, but is has no significance whatsoever.

What collectors are looking for – and this is the root of all this stick-dial-rectangular-dial stuff – is that in the last months of the 16710 Rolex assembled some scarce specimen of the GMT with the new 3186 movement that now powers the successor model 116710. And in the same period *some* models also had the rectangular dial. I repeat: some! Not all! So there is no direct correlation between the 3186 movement and the dial. Neither have all rectangular dial watches the 3186 movement nor the other way around.

However people are crazy for the rectangular dial and since someone found out that there is a stick dial also, this one is also being pushed. The truth is: whatever dial, I dare to say, whatever movement (3186 or the older 3185) the GMT has, in the long run this will make no big difference. It is a cool watch to have and in some years to come nobody will grab a lens to look at the dial to find out if its roman number 'II' is stick, rectangular or whatever else.

That's why I bought a standard GMT Pepsi with the 3185

movement, the classic one, so to say, but I bought it as a full set
and in near NOS condition, because condition and the set will
matter, will make a difference, if you ever think of reselling the
thing.

Buying it

The GMT was my first used watch. And none of the fears came
actually true. I bought it from a used watches dealer on the internet
because when if comes to used watches you deal with single pieces.
No two are alike. Every used watch has its own story and history
and that makes them indiviual. And I wanted this one. The dealer
promised the watch was as good as new, basically a safe-watch
that wasn't worn very much. It was LC100 and had the full set
with box and papers and all that really important stuff.

So I wired the money and got it.

When I showed the watch to my official Rolex dealer he looked
at it very closely and then he spoke: a very nice one. Nearly not
worn at all. No scratches, not polished, as good as new. That was
what I was looking for.

But this wonderful verdict had a very bad impact on me: what
I had there was obviously worth a lot. Perhaps even more than I
had payed for it.

The lesson from that is: if you select your dealer, do a little
internet research on his reputation, you can rely on that most of
them can be trusted. The watch world is a small community. If a
dealer sells you just one bad watch, he makes the mistake of his life,
because this information will spread on the internet like wildfire
and he probably won't sell that many watches in the future. He
success and his income might depend on his reputation. So he
in the first place will take care and make sure that the watch is
exactly what it is supposed to be.

Owning it, Wearing it

I really don't wear the GMT so much. What is a pity, as it is a really outstanding and beautiful watch. But, there are some issues.

One is that I cannot get the bracelet right for my arm. It keeps being too loose or too tight. And that might have its true cause in the weight distribution between the light (hollow link) bracelet and the watch case. Neither of it is bad, but it somehow does not fit my arm or my individual wearing habits.

Next problem is the dealer. Well, not the dealer I bought the watch from, who did an almost perfect job, but the watch dealer I brought the watch to, after the purchase to have an educated look at it.

He basically said something like: »absolutely great, near NOS condition, where on earth did you find that thing?«

From that day on I could not wear the GMT any more, because I am too afraid to damage it. Not exactly damaging and loose money but damaging a rare piece of art that are not made any more these days.

In this logic the GMT gets near to no wrist time at all because it is the most precious and scarce one of the all. I payed 7.500 for it and more and more prices tend towards $9.000 or even beyond $10.000!

Weaknesses

Did I write 'weaknesses'? Well, 'weakness' should be enough:

The GMT is kind of a one and only watch. Why do I say that? Well, here is the problem: you either wear it daily or never. Because you won't wear it with the wrong date and the GMT movement hasn't got a quick date set function.

I am not kidding. So if you don't put it on your wrist for some days, you do not only have to wind it and adjust the time, you also have to adjust the 24 hour time, which is additional fiddling, you also have to adjust the date – and that really sucks. It is a tricky one, as there is no quick date adjustment function, like in the Sub or the Datejust. No pull out the crown to position 2, set the date by rotating the crown and then go on with daily business. Neither in the 3185 nor in the recent 3186 movement.

So what you basically do then is, use the hour adjustment function of the GMT movement to quickly rotate the hour hand round and round and round until the date reaches the right position. That is not very comfortable at all.

However, would I purchase the GMT again?

Yes, of course, because since I bought it (today some 6 months ago) its price already went up for about $1500. No, just kidding. No.

Yes, I would because it is a perfect piece and in my opinion more of a Rolex icon than the Daytona. Without at GMT you are just not a complete man. It is so masculine that it even compensates the Yachtmaster's image.

State of the Collection

Rolex has two icons: the Sub and the Daytona. Yes, but today, there is another one: the GMT Master II 16710 Pepsi. Rolex managed to make their third icon by: first, stopping its production after about 50 basically unchanged years and, second, replacing it by a model that not everyone likes, and, third, making a Pepsi in whitegold that is not priced for everyones purse.

The result: a run for the old discontinued 16710, without the Supercase, without the whitegold but with everything that made this watch a legend for over 5 decades. That's how you make an icon. And of course with Pussy Galore in the early days.

Figure 8.2: Not another diver, but a pilot's watch: GMT Master II 16710.

Chapter 9

What makes a Man?

»What makes a man Mr. Lebowski? Is it to do anything necessary to achieve?«

»Yea, that and a pair of testicles.«

When we were little boys we all liked the same things: fast supercars like the Lamborghini Countach, fast planes like the SR-71 Blackbird and huge dinosaurs like the Brachiosaurus and of course the T-Rex.

Why? Because they are top notch, superlatives, king of the hill, spectacular numbers, 300 km/h, 3600 km/h, 100 tons of living flesh. Huge impressive numbers. Being a boy is all about being on top. Some men forgot that over time, but boys know it quite well.

Being associated to these top achieving things, we felt also top notch, we felt being the superlative ourselves. In card games it was *our* Countach that had that top speed compared to the other, lesser cards, it was *our* Blackbird and our T-Rex. Well, at least we had the right card in our little hands.

Boys really like superlatives as they are very competitive. To compete in all fields and areas of their existence is their elixir of live, is the essence of their being. To be better, to be the alpha-male guarantees them to reproduce if you think about it on an evolutionary scale. So they have fun, when they win. Noting else matters. Because it impresses the girls.

And today? We are still the same boys, with, well, some

features added, but no basic changes.

So we still like superlatives although they became a bit more subtle. We now apreciate the ellegance of a decent Aston Martin, the fascination of a simple plane for its ability to fly and the top predator T-Rex is just being replaced by another top notch predator: a Rolex Sea-Dweller or a AP Royal Oak Offshore.

We don't have card games any more, but try to drive the Aston, wear the AP, be the pilot of the plane.

Watch sizes to wear...

... to be a real man. Size does matter – if you are still a boy.

So naturally, the watch a grown up boy wears must be bigger than that of the other boy across the table. That is as obvious as no *woman* will ever have any other cause for the size of *her* watch, than fashion. If it is bigger than the other woman's watch? Who cares?

Men. They care. So sizes of watches went up recently – one could argue, since grown up luxury watches (that for ages had been a privilege of the upper class) are more and more worn by grown up boys (from the upper middle class).

So watches (not the boys) went up from a normal size of 36 mm case diameter for a very very long time (basically since the war) to the in those days considered large size of 40 mm during the 1970s to 1990s when sports watches became more and more the dress watches of our times and now went to 44 mm recently.

That trend of course has many fathers. There is of course the fact that people get bigger. The nutritious and protein rich food in the first world countries lets people become significantly larger than some decades ago. In middle Europe e.g. the average height of a male went from 1.67 m at the beginning of the 20th century to an average of 1.80 one hundred years later. 13 cm don't sound like much until you stand next to a man that is 1.67 cm. And the fact that the average size changed from 1.63 to 1.67 (4 cm) since 5000 BC and from 1900 to 2000 from 1.67 to 1.80 (13 cm) puts this a bit more into perspective. And concerning watches: bigger guys naturally have bigger wrists and for that reason alone need bigger sized watches to not look ridiculous.

Then there is fashion. Since the luxury watch world became a mass phenomenon in the last 25 years, it also became more and more a subject to the laws of fashion. And the most basic rule of fashion is still, don't do the same thing again as last year, because people never want what they already have but they as sure as hell continuously want, what they don't have. So clearly, there are watchmakers that subdue themselves to that rules (like Hublot) and others like Rolex or Panerai who don't. They set trends or remain basically silent and unmoved by the noise of the world.

So if you make the trend like Panerai did with its 44 and 48 mm watch designs derived from their true military tool watches of the 1930s and 1940s, or if you just try everything to attract attention like Hublot does, you are basically in the fashion market. And that market just says, be louder than the rest – and for that matter bigger in the first place. And if people have 36 and 40 mm watches and are satisfied with them, offer them 44 and 48 mm specimen and tell them, that they need one of those to be trendy – or for that matter be cool as the military guys with their hard faces who always wore those Breitling 46 or 50 mm things over their pilots' overalls.

I am an engineer. And so my suspicion is that there is another reason for that trend: that the bigger sized watches are easier to make and are more robust at the same time. Think of it: in a 44 or 46 mm watch case with a height of 16 or 20 mm you can fit a much larger movement than in a significantly smaller case, like 36 mm and 6 mm height. And in this watchmaking world of near micro-technology, where parts are often easily thinner than a hair, it makes a huge difference if you can make your parts a little larger. They not only handle better when you assemble the movement, because they will not all be gone when you sneeze once, they also will be more robust and hence the whole movement will be. I think that is the reason why Rolex put large pocket-watch movements into the military watches they shipped to Panerai in the 1930s. They were very rugged, because they were huge.

And in times when every watchmaker like Hublot, Panerai, Breitling, IWC and all the others try to become real manufacturers who make everything themselves, especially the movements, like the icons of Rolex, Patek, AP, Vacheron and Jaeger-LeCoultre do for ages, there it might come handy if you don't have to cram your newly developed movement into a 36 or 34 mm case. Yes I think not only the market demand wants bigger watches, but also the watchmakers try to inspire the market in that direction.

Of course there are other ways to be the T-Rex. Rolex e.g. does only very reluctantly take part in that sort of game. In the Rolex case the crown on the dial is enough to feel being the T-Rex. The Patek owner pretends to be not interested in that sort of game at all, basically because he already *is* the T-Rex for a very long time.

So is it necessary to wear a 44 mm military watch to be a man?

My opinion? No, not really. For me the best watch size is 40 mm and I really love my 36 mm Explorer. And I am a big guy of 1.90 m height and athletic 100 kg. But 36 fits my wrist as well as 40. I can also wear a Big Bang or a Luminor Marina, no problem. But I like the 40 size or the 42 of the Speedmaster, because it is very comfortable and fits under every cuff. And I especially like the 36 mm Ex as it is subtle and distinguished and cool more than all the other hulking high tech guys.

Chapter 10

Explore a Bit More

I finally accepted that I had become a Rolex fan. Something I had never expected had come true.

But as I understood now, the simple truth is that the success of Rolex is based mainly on two simple facts: their watches are technically brillant and probably the best on the market. Rolex focuses obviously on the right things people appreciate: reliability, continuity, value. No experiments, no nonsense, no extravagance.

That's all. That's what makes great products.

The Style of an Era

I always thought that there was a literal similarity between the Explorer and the Panerai style watches. The polished bezel, the dark dial with the reduced hour markers and the large numbers.

Somehow one seemed to resemble the other. Although both have nothing to do with each other, right?

Wrong.

Well, we'll come back to that later...

The Good, the Bad and the Ugly Watchmakers

There are at least three kinds of swiss luxury watchmakers: manufacturers, watchmakers and... well, brands.

Let me explain that a bit. A manufacturer is the most renown kind. A manufacturer does everything himself. Any decision of make-or-buy he answers with 'make'. So the depth of his production is outstanding. That means, he makes the cases of (most of) his watches, he makes his bracelets, he makes his dials, his hands, his hour markers, ... you get the idea.

All that does also the watchmaker. But the manufacturer does more. He of course makes his own movements. Only a watchmaker who makes his own movements for his watches may be called a manufacturer. He designs his movements, he builds them and they work pretty well.

Because this is the whole point of makeing everything yourself instead of buying: the control you get, in order to produce outstanding quality, perfection. If you source parts you don't have perfect control. You get bad parts, you get suboptimal parts and you cannot do a lot about it. The only thing you can do is making the part yourself.

Rolex goes completely mad in this case. Rolex even makes their own stainless steel in their own foundary. They make their own gold alloys from raw gold. They try to make absolutely everything themselves, in order to have as much control as possible – and of course building a legend for their marketing department also. The result is legendary ruggedness and precision of the core parts of their watches: the movements. The result is being on top of the self.

And there is another aspect that differentiate the manufacturers: a lot of Swiss watchmakers belong to large companies. They are part of luxury holdings like Richmond or Swatch. They of course benefit from that economic power in their back but on the other hand are they no longer completely free to do what they find necessary. When there is a large maker of movements in the company, it will be hard for them to invest a lot of money in making their own movements. Nobody wants them to reinvent the wheel. That is inefficient, that costs a lot of money.

There are not very many free companies left, like Rolex, who form their own group together with Tudor, or like Patek Philippe.

These are considered the creme de la creme of Swiss watchmaking, basically because their products are of outstanding quality.

Then there are the companies that are there for a very long time with an unbroken lineage and heritage and manage incresingly to hold steady despite being part of a large holding, like Omega, Breguet, A. Lange, Jaeger-LeCoultre and of course the Holy Trinity member Vacheron Constantin.

But then there are the mere brands, a history but without the unbroken lineage. They are brands that are owned by the big companies that basically intend to make money with the sound of the brand name and their already finished historical importance. Names of companies that are long gone or have been completely replaced and are mere brands with indistinguishable production in the background. The result of this phaenomenon are watches that are called TAG Heuer, Longines, Hamilton or Panerai, but they basically don't have anything to do with their identically named ancestors. And all these watches are all basically the same. They all use the same movements from ETA in different looking cases. That does not necessarily mean that they are bad watches. But they are a little bit of the shelf, but for a premium price. Of course all those brands try to become real watchmakers and even manufacturers but this is a long way to got and there are no shortcuts.

And of course the market where a lot of knowledgable people are around, reflects this situation. The real value of these watches can be found in their resale value, when they are used. While used watches from manufacturers and the very good watchmakers are constant in their value over very long time spans, what means that they are valued very high also when they are 10 or 20 years old, basically because their level of quality is so high that their products function perfectly even after 20 or 40 or even 100 years.

The cheaper watchmakers that work with ETA movements aren't bad either, but they are considered much worse than the manufacturers and so their value diminishes over the decades as their usability also decreases. That of course does not mean that these are bad watches. They only aren't considered immortal like the top notch brands.

And that there is a lot of truth in that, can be shown by another detail: the Omega Speedmaster. It is one of the few Omega watches that also keep their value over time and even increase with every new price round of Omega. Why? Because it went to the moon? No probably not. The Speedmaster Profesional was made by Omega in the early 1960s to become the NASA space watch. And how did they do the trick? The just selected not a ETA or ETA based movement, but they selected the movement that was considered the best chronograph movment of that time: the chronograph movement from Lemania. A company that made and designed formidable movements and shipped them also to Breitling and Patek Philippe. If you'd put it rather blunt, the Speedy in that sense is kind of a Patek with a Omega case. Is that enough to be something special?

So here again, the quality of the movement decides a lot when it comes to value. Because the Speedy does not use the typical Omega movements, but one you normaly find in a Patek. And the monetary value of these watches just reflect that.

So to have fun and not loose money (a lot of money, if we are talking luxury watches), you better stick to the manufacturers and the very good makers like Breitling and Omega. And never buy the brands. They are also decent watches (well, sort of), but they will loose you money.

But keep in mind: what a simple brand characterizes is *not* bad watches. It is 1) watches that, based on their brand name *pretend* to be more than they really are. They are pretending to have a heritage and a lineage that is not really there. 2) for that reason their retail price is much higher than their true value is. Their true value can be found if you compare the used price to the retail price. If the maker would charge a realistic price for these watches, a lot of things would be ok with them.

The thing is that these brands are often brands of formidable watchmakers from another time that simply ceased to exist, they went out of business; the brand then was bought by a large company who now start to make watches using that brand – watches that obviously have nothing to do with the original company, because that originality is often based on a single person or a team of watchmakers that trade their wisdom to the next generation. But if you break this tradition by getting out of business, all that is left is a nice memory of great watches. That way they may still have the same brand name, but the way they are making their watches is completely changed.

E.g. Panerai in the 1930s did not really make their own watches. They more or less assembled watch parts together and printed their name on them. Panerai watches from that era were completely made by Rolex and shipped to Italy, where they were given to the Italian Navy as Panerai diving watches – why they are very sought after today in the first place. So if Panerai today says that they made watches in the 1930s this is basically not true. Not true in the sense that Panerai watches of today had anything literal to do with the watches of the past era. And not in the sense that Panerai basically in the important era from 1936 to 1956 did not make watches at all, but used a completely ready Rolex design, made and shipped by Rolex to Italy as their product.

And today's Panerai has completely moved to Switzerland and you can be sure that nobody of the Italians that made Panerai products in the 1930s has anything to do with the Swiss guys who make Panerai watches today. The only constant here is the brand name. Basically, Richemont bought the name and then made fancy watches inspired by the original Panerai / Rolex design from the 1930s to 1950s. This is not heritage, of course not lineage, this is a brand name and a completely new product that *looks* like the old product. If there was any heritage at all, Panerai should be completely made by Rolex, that would at least have some historical importance and significance – and of course on the price and the value of the watches. So if Rolex bought Panerai and now the Rolex Group would consist of Rolex, Tudor and Panerai, that would make some sense. But the way it is, Panerai today simply pretends to be something they completely are not. They are a brand.

But don't confuse that with cheaper watches. There are a lot of cheaper watches around, that do not have this problem: e.g. a Seiko for 300 bucks is not a bad watch in any respect. It is a quality product from Japan that is just very reasonably priced. You get a watch for 300 bucks that is worth every penny. It is a honest product that does not try to pretend something it isn't. The problem with these brand watches is that they charge the premium price of a premium product for a standard quality product at best. The Seiko doesn't do that. It says it is a quality product and it has a quality product price. Nothing wrong with that.

In that sense also the Hublot Big Bang is kind of a rip off. Obviously it is a design clone of the Audemars-Piguet classic Royal Oak Offshore which is around since about 1992. Hublot took this iconic and cool design language in the mid 2000s, made it even fancier, combining it with a rubber strap, using fancy materials, put a rather cheap ETA movement in it and charged a premium price, even a little over-premium price, for a rather premium looking product, that is basically a simple watch. It still isn't a Royal Oak, but it costs nearly as much.

Unexpected Siblings

I always thought that there was a literal similarity between the Explorer and the Panerai style watches. The polished bezel, the dark dial with the reduced hour markers and the large numbers.

Somehow one seemed to resemble the other. Although both have nothing to do with each other, right?

That similarity is not by accident of course. The classic Explorer design was conceived in the 1940s and that was just 5 years after Rolex began shipping their real first diving watch (which wasn't the Sub) to Italy, where these watches magically became watches made by Officine Panerai.

So the simiar design just shows that the Panerai design and the Explorer are closely related siblings. Besides their dimensions of course: the Ex with 36 mm and the Panerai being the classic oversized watch with 44 and even 46 mm diameter.

Figure 10.1: Siblings: Rolex Explorer and Panerai Militare

Before the Purchase

Of course I did not for a second consider buying the new model with the 39 mm diameter case. But that was quickly over when I had the 36 mm version on my wrist. Beauty. I saw it on my wrist and that was it. The only question was, where to buy it as the one I had on my wrist was without box and papers, what I did not want.

Figure 10.2: Rolex Explorer Ref. 114270 (36 mm) and 214270 (39 mm)

Again it proved to be not so dangerous at all to buy a used watch as I at first feared. I found an appropriate specimen on a dealers website for a good price.

What I did next was trying to find out the dealer's reputation. So I looked on my favourite watch enthusiast internet forum for the name of the dealer and found only good reviews. One thread was even a congratulation threat for the dealer (obviously a one-man-show-company) to his birthday and a lot of the guys in the forum called him by his first name (what is much more uncommon in Germany, than in english speaking countries and basically means that there is some kind of friendship like relation between the people).

So I looked in Google search for the dealers name and combined it with 'problem', 'trust' and other keywords and everything I could find was praise.

Ok then.

So I first reserved the watch, that he would not sell it to someone else, as the dealer was in another city some 100 miles away. Then I went there on the next possible occasion, about 8 days later.

I found myself in his home office. A very friendly guy who very open and clear showed me the watch and told me everthing about it, the good, the bad and the ugly (which wasn't there at all).

I decieded to buy it. We did all the formalities and then he said, wait a second. Then he came back with some excerpts from his private collection: a 1970s plastic Submariner. Another beautiful 1610 Explorer. It quickly became a talk between watch aficionados, friends due to the hobby and passion they share.

Owning it, wearing it

The *small* Explorer is an unbelivably balanced watch. The (rattlesnake) Oyster bracelet is sporty, while the polished steel bezel is classy. The dial is decent, while the 3 6 9 hour makers make it a bit more sporty again. The 36 mm case makes it very distinguished and subtle, while its stance as a very robust mountaineers watch has nothing of the sensibilities of a true dress watch. The Ex 1 is just perfect in every way, shape and form and works in every environment you can possibly think of.

The Rolex Explorer nearly became my exitwatch. But as we

Figure 10.3: Rolex Explorer Ref. 114270 (2008)

afficionados know: the idea of an exit watch is just another strategy to purchase another watch.

So this wasn't at all what I had in mind, when I got my Rolex Explorer.

I of course bought the youngtimer 114270, the last one with the for over 60 years classical 36 mm Oyster case, not the latest less elegant bulky 39 mm incarnation 214270.

I obviously was swimming against the tide from larger to smaller watches. Everybody who thinks he needs a hulking 44 mm watch should also look at some of these smaller ones, just because, he might be altogether wrong.

Today, as I am writing this down, wearing a Explorer, I would say, there are two reasonable watch sizes: normal = 36 mm and oversized sports = 40 mm. Everything else is too big – or too small.

That sounds a little bit old fashioned, but I say: time is on my side. For over 70 years, this was the golden rule of watchmaking in terms of case sizes and just because some fashion models like the Hublot Big Bang, the Panerai Remakes and the Breitling oversized along with the traditionally huge IWC pilot's watch models have some fans these days, does not mean that this way older rule of rules of watch sizes might be wrong.

To be honest, I never quite understood those Explorer I 36 mm fanboys. Now I can.

Figure 10.4: Dresswatch and Sports watch all-in-one: Rolex Explorer 114270

Glowing from Within

The Explorer 1 has a peculiar magic dark inner glow to it. In certain light situations, the brushed steel has an almost dark grey shade, much darker than other watches with the same finish. This looks even more elegant than the usual steel color. It is almost magical.

These days (it is October now) the 114270 Explorer I is becoming my daily wearer. It wears so light, elegant and beautiful. It fits under every sleeve or cuff, it's practical, decent, wearable at any occation, in short: it is a perfect watch. However, what else would you expect from a design that has been only slightly optimized for more than 5 decades!

Funny thing is: at my first contact with a Rolex retailer, the guy indeed recommended the Explorer I to me as a great watch

Figure 10.5: Magical dark glow: Rolex Explorer 114270

for a beginner. However, so close and yet so far, as it was 2015, he of course meant the 39 mm 214270. And that would of course have been the 39 mm, the *wrong* one. He showed it to me and my ignorant reaction back then was that it didn't pop enough for my liking. I found it too decent, not masculine and sporty enough. Very clever indeed.

This shows two things: you need to learn what is good for you – and that process takes some time to gain a certain level and then of course basically never ends. And part of that learning process is that you sometimes must have things, only to find out that you don't need them.

If you now believe that I consider my Sea-Dweller a mistake because I found out that I don't really need it, you are wrong. You are not expected to love only one watch. These are watches, not women.

The Mercedes Star

Some people tend to laugh about the 'mercedes star' the typical Rolex marking of the hour hand. Basically it looks a bit odd, that a luxury brand like Rolex features a structure on their products that looks like to logo of another luxury brand: that of german car maker Mercedes-Benz.

But that is all not so peculiar at all, as this is just coincidence and the Rolex 'Mercedes star' has absolutely nothing to do with the car maker logo.

Tool watches are not primarily about aesthetics, but about usability. And for something that is supposed to show the time usability has a lot to do with readability.

If you look at a watch with two hands you usually can tell the hour by the orientation of the short hand and the minute by the long hand. But a problem arises, when both hands point to exactly the same direction. Then, as you normally recognize the time without thinking so much, you just miss the hour hand. Where is it? You don't think 'oh yea the hour hand is behind the minute hand, so it's probably... you tend to think 'where the f* is that b* hour hand. It's gone' before you of course recognize that it is *not* gone but behind the minute hand.

The Omega Speedmaster is a candidate for that kind of thought train.

However, this already is way too much thinking. You need to instantly recognize the time. Everything else costs too much time in a e.g. critical situation, be it under water or on top of a mountain or in a meeting, whenever time is a matter of life and death a tool simply shouldn't make you think – before you can act.

So with a Rolex watch you never are in such a situation, because you always can find the hour hand – due to the 'Mercedes star' on the hour hand introduced back then with the Rolex Explorer.

By the way: the 'Mercedes star' probably is not a 'Mercedes star' at all, but a little symbol for the dial with the three hands of the watch.

Weakness

Yes, even the iconic, beloved, wonderful Explorer has a weakness: (and this is a simple one, as you might expect from a gloriously simplistic watch) you never know, what day it is. It has no date.

This is not the worst weakness on the planet, and with a date it wouldn't be so perfectly balanced and would become something like a Datejust, what nobody wants. And because of the tiny date window necessary in a 36 mm watch, it then inevitably would need a Cyclops lense and that would spoil it completely. So this is just one of those weaknesses, that you have to accept, because there is no cure for it and thus should simply be just worn with pride.

Would I purchase the Explorer again:

Oh yes! I love it that much that I indeed dearly would like to also have its simpler predecessor the 1016 – although it is basically more or less the same watch! And today way too expensive.

State of the Watch Collection

This is now becoming more and more a Rolex Collection. Adding the Explorer I 114270, the collection now has 4 Rolex pieces one Omega and one Panerai. But again the latest Rolex piece is not a diver but a Explorer, a mountaineer's and adventurer's watch with outstanding ruggedness and reliability.

Figure 10.6: Added an Ex I Ref. 114270

Chapter 11

Vintage or just Old

In my opinion you have to accept in which time you are living.

Yes of course the 1016 Explorer from 1988 is a total beauty. And the 1972 1655 Orange Hand Explorer II in my book, is clearly more beautiful than any of its successors. And the 1965 6265 Daytona is a true classic. And the 1960 James Bond 6538 Sub is just brillant. All that is true, but...

Keep in mind what these watches are – besides being highly collectible and sought after like hell: they are old, sometimes really heavily worn and – *and* – often not a very good watch in the first place by today's standards. Even when they were new, they were tool watches meant to be worn, used, busted and replaced by the next one.

Compared to what newer models from the modern era have to offer, they often lack certain technological enhancements. They weren't exactly cheap in their times but they were not luxury watches. A luxury watch in that era was made of gold. These steel pieces plainly were only tool watches.

And even if the tool watch today got something like an advancement and is considered a respectable class of watches, back in the day, a tool watch was something like a screwdriver. Use it and when it's broken thow it away and buy a new one.

And some, like the Daytonas didn't even have an inhouse Rolex movement as Rolex back then sourced a ETA chronograph movement for their only chronograph. The Daytona, the only chronograph they made then, they designed to compete at NASA for the space missions (why it was called 'Cosmograph' in the first place)... but they lost that to Omega. And the better Omega Speedmaster with the famous Lemania movement became the one and only original NASA space and finally Moon watch. And so the 'Rolex Cosmograph' lay in the shops like lead and they changed its name and its purpose to race driving and so it was called the 'Daytona' after the famous American race track. It really did not do so well: I just saw a beautiful, nowadays $30,000 Daytona that was actually produced in 1971 and sold by the dealer in 1978!

Figure 11.1: real classics: Rolex 1016 Explorer, 1655 Explorer II, 6562 Daytona

That kind of a lesser demand back in these days is of course part of the scarcity of these models today: as nobody wanted them back then, Rolex did not make a lot and today there are not very many around what makes them so collectible and people are willing to pay $30,000 to even $150,000 for basically an old and worn steel Rolex case and even more worn out steel bracelet with a not so brillant ETA movement that didn't even succeed to go to the Moon.

We have to assess: this is not the price for a watch, because the watch obviously isn't worth it by any means. This is the price for a piece of art, which is of course highly irrational. We do not really talk about watches in such a case any more, but about pieces of art where the price is now completely detached from the use value or the material value or the value of workmanship to reproduce such a piece today. In this situation the price is completely ideational and does not root in any rational explanation any more.

You can of course pay that sort of money for other works of art. A picture from the early 1900s has not even a function, is larger and more delicate to any sort of damage than a robust steel watch. But will that watch be considered a precious treasure in another 50 years or so like e.g. some Picasso pencil sketches for the same money? I don't know that.

So should you really pay tens of thousands of Dollars for a 50 year old steel watch? In my opinion, if you have been lucky enough to have bought a Daytona in 1970 for $400 or a 1016 Explorer for $250 and you were clever enough to keep it over time despite the heavily increasing prices, you just have one of those beautiful icons and you can be proud of them – good for you.

If you weren't able to pick up such a brillant piece, should you buy one of those today? In my opinion: no. I wouldn't pay $10,000 or even $30,000 for scrap metal. I find it often hard to accept to pay $15,000 for a brand new steel watch, like a Royal Oak, or even better for a plastic watch like a AP Forged Carbon or the Hublot Big Bang Carbon. But these are at least new or nearly new watches with brillant movements and the highest reputation.

Figure 11.2: materials: AP Royal Oak Steel, Royal Oak Offshore Forged Carbon, Hublot Big Bang Unico Carbon

In my opinion the steel luxury watch itself is a trick. AP with its Royal Oak has played this trick on the buyers and has been copied by the other watchmakers ever since. The trick is: charge a premium price for a cheap steel thing.

Until the Royal Oak, a luxury watch for a luxury price tag was made of gold. It was a scandal, when AP presented the Royal Oak not only being a provocative design, but made from steel for a luxury price. Why they made it is clear: the cost for the material drops from today around $5000 to $1. The remaining $4999 are your additional earnings. The fool is the buyer.

Don't get me wrong. Of course steel is a great material for a watch. It is much more scratch resistant than all the precious metals, it is not too heavy, like the previous metals are, it can resist pressure and chemical attacks (like sweat or salt water) and it is brilliantly customizable, as steel is an alloy that can be given a lot of different properties by mixing the right portions of chrome, mangan and nickel and some others into it. This all is very well scientifically studied and steel is even easy to manufacture and you can even make the surface harder by additional manufacturing steps. It's a brillant technical material.

But on the other hand: if you pay $20,000 for a gold watch you have at least bought (if you forget that whole watch and time measurement thing for a moment) let's say about 100 to 200 grams of gold, which is today worth about $5,000 for the gold alone. If you consider the value of the same mass of steel, you have basically $1 in your hands. And that is the trick I was talking about. Buying a gold watch you have bought some gold – at least. Buying a steel watch you have, if everything goes wrong, bought some scrap metal.

But what about the sought after vintage watches? As I see it, it is hard to find a really good one. Often the case and the plastic crystal and the bracelet are very worn – they were relatively cheap tool watches back then, remember, so they were used and worn and busted – and probably so is the movement as the movement usually is as worn as the case (for obvious reasons, when you think about it). The dial often has massive traces of radioactive damage, especially the hands and hour markers and thus it is not but *was* radioactive does not loom any more in the dark. Let's say it like it is: they are old, they are partly disfunctional and it can be a real pain to find and pay for a spare repair part for that long discontinued movement.

Of course these old pieces are beautiful and if you have them and have bought them for a good price some 10 or 20 years ago, good for you. If you don't, well, I for one admire them, I love them from a distance, but I put my 10 or 20 grand in some newer models that are not worn, have modern inhouse calibers and despite that reason are much cheaper.

How New is Used

If I buy a used watch I prefer it to be younger than or at least around 10 years.

Additionally I try to make my homework, which production years exactly have the features that I want. E.g. there are several newer versions of the 16710 GMT Pepsi: there are the dial variations 'normal', 'stick dial' and the 'rectangle dial'. But these differences you can hardly see with the naked eye came into the spot light because there was also a version of the 16710 with the new 3136 movement and some of these had the rectangular dial. But not all of them. And one thing was clear to the expert: the old model with the new movement will be a collectors item, as there are not many and it was the best of both worlds: the old case and the up-to-date movement. Today the 3136 GMT is sold for $10,000 to $20,000 while the 16710 GMT with the older 3135 movement in good condition is more like $8,000.

So if I would want to invest that kind of money, I'd go for the 3136 version. However, this model is already so expensive that I just got the normal version in good condition from 2004.

I have a natural tendency to become more and more unwilling to buy a watch older than 10 or 15 years. And if a watch is older than 20 years it must be a real special piece. And a watch older than 30 or 40 years is usually so expensive or so busted (or both) that I simply don't see the connection between the price and the piece anymore.

Of course there is the lore that a Rolex, esp. the movement is so robust that it will life longer than you, what means that a 50 year old Rolex just spent half of its estimated lifetime. I don't buy into that completely. Yes Rolex makes excellent movements that run with outstanding precision: the standard Submariner, Sea-Dweller, Yachtmaster, Deep-Sea 3135 movement that Rolex makes for over 30 years now, is meanwhile so perfect that it does not go wrong for 2 seconds a day, what the COSC test demands, but 2 seconds a *week*! If you have the watch on the wrist and it thus runs at about 35 degrees C skin temperature. That is of course outstanding precision.

But even if you reduce wear inside the movement by using friction minimal and extremely hard materials, you cannot avoid wear completely. And you cannot avoid damage of the movement by hard blows. Obviously even one of those magical Rolex movements need to be serviced every 5 to 10 years or so. And that is the case because there definitely is wear.

You can of course service a watch movement like you would service a plane: you just replace every part that can fail way before the end of its expected lifetime. That is basically one of the puzzle pieces why planes almost never crash due to mechanical failure: all the mechanical parts of a plane are always brand new, even if the plane was first built 10 or 80 years ago. So they don't fail.

You can of course do that with a watch. But I doubt that this would be a bargain. And like the plane you will not have the same movement after some years but a completely updated new one. And this is also not what the collectors want.

And someday the uttermost extreme thing happens: you send the watch to Rolex for a service and they send it back, without being serviced, because they have no spare parts left for that model. Recently I heard from a collector who was befallen by that gruesome fate. The watch was a 6562 and Rolex refused to service it. A watch that probably had cost him several tenth of thousands! Of course the watch can be still used even if it is not serviced. But the end of this watch life comes in sight. And with it the price of these models will definitely never be the same again. And in that case it is totally clear why Rolex decided to do that. The watch not even has a Rolex movement. For a Rolex inhouse movement they probably have the means to make parts themselves. But not in that case. These parts, gone for once, are not in stock any more. And that's the end.

Rolex even stated that they will discontinue servicing all the plastic crystal models over time. They probably will do so to disrupt the huge Rolex vintage market, that definitely costs them a lot of money as people today tend to decide to buy a used Rolex instead of a now one. Just because the older models are considered more elegant than the newer ones.

I think old watches are really a hype. It is nice to have them but if you don't, love them from a distance. You can of course do the things your way. These are just my 2 cents.

Chapter 12

Watch from the Moon

Have you ever been on the Moon? Me? Not even close.

The Omega Speedmaster Professional definitely deserves the 'Professional', as this is the one and only watch NASA to this day gives their astronauts to wear on their space missions. Not only the Apollo astronauts way back then in the time got one, also todays' Space Shuttle and Space Station missions also rely in last instance, in case every electronical device and every computer ceases function, on the Speedmaster Professional – I doubt this would help today, but lore tells us that at least in the Apollo 13 case the Speedy saved the life of the three astronauts. Be it so or not, it is definitely a professional tool watch, more than many other watches that merely try to be one.

Indeed I never had the Omega Speedmaster Professional Moonwatch on my wrist before. Seriously. I knew for half of my life, that I needed a chronograph, I already had considered it being my first proper wristwatch, but the opportunity never surfaced to test the Speedy live and in technicolor. Never in my life. Isn't that peculiar when you think about it being it the first 'real' wristwatch that caught my attention way way back in the 1980s?

I once had the opportunity to look at a Speedmaster Reduced (who on earth seriously wants a watch that is called 'Reduced'?) but I neither put it on my wrist nor did it catch on, I simply didn't like that one very much. It looked smallish to me, too many functions and registers crammed into a too small dial. And for that reason not very elegant at all.

I finally put the Speedmaster Professional with its 42 mm case on my wrist in a watch shop in early 2016. And it took me about half a second to recognize: this original Speedy is an utter beauty. On the Top Gear Cool Wall it would definitely belong into 'Sub Zero' (that's cooler than 'seriously cool'). No doubt about that.

But only if you see it live. The Speedy has a strange way of not being photogenic at all. On a photo it often seems to not sitting perfectly on the wrist or being somewhat too large. It often seems too black or too simple or all of it at once. If you put it on your wrist that is all not the case. It indeed wears perfect. And that is because it is quite light.

Understanding it

Of course it is a vintage piece. The Speedy Moonwatch is basically a vintage watch from the 1960s you can still buy new. It is like NOS, New Old Stock, without the Old Stock. The Speedmaster Professional is a kind of vintage watch because it is made for nearly 60 years now without any (visible) change – and also not very much invisible changes, because once certified by NASA in 1963 you cannot change anything without loosing your certification.

The first Speedmaster was made in 1957. And only a couple of years later it went to NASA to compete with other chronographs of that time about which one of them would be taken to the moon.

So obviously design and bling was never an important issue for the Speedy. And that is of course because it is a real tool watch. It is supposed to have been worn in space and perhaps even on the moon (if really someone went there in the late 60s) and so you should not expect a lot of bling like whitegold indeces or an overly shiny bracelet like its contestant at NASA, the Rolex 'Cosmograph' has them. It is a space watch, not jewelry.

Even if I doubt that the Speedmaster watches actually visited the moon, it still is a respectable piece of technology as it was and is certified by NASA for all the other spaceflights with the

Space Shuttle and the International Space Station (ISS) as well. The Speedy is definitely a piece of equipment used in real space missions and even outside of spacecrafts in spacewalk missions.

But why do they use the Speedy even today? Wouldn't a quartz watch be more precise? Well, yes and no. The Speedmaster on the wrist of an astronaut is something like his las instrument, when all the other fail. On Apollo 13 this worked out quite well, when the whole computer of the Apollo module was knocked out of the game. And then you simply need a different kind of system, when all the electronics fail, you need to rely on a mechanical computer. In space this might even be better than any quartz chip watch: because of the deep space radiation. Mechanical movements survive even a severe impact of high power radiation, what no electronical device would.

And if that wasn't already enough merits for a simple watch, the astronauts' Omega Speedmasters on Apollo 13 also played an important role in saving the three astronauts' lifes. Apollo 13 got into trouble (as the lore goes) in deep space half way to the moon and they had to navigate their way back to earth mainly without a lot of help from their shutdown computer. So they timed e.g. how long their rocket engines had to deliver thrust with their Omega Speedmasters. Their lives depending on the quality of their Omega watches, working in that harsh environment properly and reliable. Sounds a bit too good to be true, a bit like made up in the marketing department. But that's just my opinion.

You often hear that the movement of the original Speedmaster Moonwatch was a 'Lemania' based movement. Besides the fact that I find this name very peculiar, as it is just one Letter (A) away from A-Lemania, Alemania = Germany in southern Europe languages), the question arises, what that is, Lemania?

What you find out is that Lemania is a most renown developer and manufacturer of movements, founded in 1884 by a former watch-maker of 'the watchmaker of the watchmakers' Jaeger-LeCoultre (see Luxury Watches). He got a lot of attention and even prizes for his movements and the company was considered as one of the finest suppliers of chronograph movements of the 20th century. Early versions of the Breitling Navitimer had a Lemania chronograph movement and even Patek Philippe used Lemania movements in some of their watches – and what more can you say to ennoble a watch industry supplier.

So obviously, when Omega got their request from NASA to provide a chronograph suitable for space missions, they did not hesitate to put the best chronograph movement they could think of into their contestant for NASA. A movement that was complicated to manufacture but technically top notch and very very robust and reliable.

And that way they created a classic. To this day the Lemania-based movement is a hard thing to manufacture, but the heritage and the marketing image the Speedmaster Moonwatch creates for Omega, is just priceless.

The Decision

This was an easy one to decide. When I first had the Speedy on my wrist I looked down at it and that was it. It was an immediate purchase. It never was as clear as that: you definitely need a Speedy Pro.

Purchasing it

Buy used or new? As the 'vintage' models Speedmaster Professional is still available as a brand new version, the question arose to buy it used or new.

When I purchased it, I broke rule No. 1 of ArchieLuxury that is: never buy retail. But I did. And that was because of four reasons:

Firstly, I want a perfect watch, not some worn down old thing. And the Speedy Moonwatch was available retail, so why settle with less.

Secondly, a eight year old used Speedy was only $400 less (about 10%). That is a good thing, when you lateron should decide to sell it, because it obviously has the ability to keep its value. But if you only save 400 bucks if you take the risk of buying used, I decided, if I have to pay nearly full retail price for the used one, I put my money into the new, untouched one. That way I also completely avoided the risk of accidentally receiving a fake watch.

Thirdly, the Speedy is a watch you do wear. You can buy a used watch if it is in good condition and for the most time of its existence lived in a bank vault. Such a watch is as good as new, neither the case is worn (what you can see), even more important, because you cannot see it directly, also the movement should not be worn. The more expensive a watch is, the higher is the probability that the owner wore it only seldomly and at occations that did not do any harm to it (like a wedding, visiting the opera and that kind of thing – if you do not clap extensively in the end, that is). The Speedy is not so expensive at all. It is a watch you can and should wear.

Fourth, of course you *must* buy used, if the watch is not in production any more as are the most iconic Rolex watches, like the 16710 GMT, the 114270 Explorer or the 16520 Daytona. In these cases you have no choise. But with the Speedy you have.

So I got the new one.

Owning it, Wearing it

And then you have it. First thing you notice: the Speedy wears quite comfortably on the wrist. It wears light, even compared to its wet sibling the James Bond Seamaster Professional.

But being a space watch it us totally appropriate that the Speedmaster is quite lightweight. There is a saying in engineering that in the vehicle industry every additional kilogram costs $100, in aviation it costs $1000 and in spaceflight $10000. This is what it costs to bring 1 kilogram of equipment to where it needs to be to do its job. So even if the Speedy weighs just 100 gramms it is totally conform to everything that matters in space techology that it is a comparably lightweight watch. Nothing else would be appropriate.

This of course is due to the crystal. Instead of glas or sapphire,

Figure 12.1: cuff-able: Omega Speedmaster Professional (2016)

that can burst into tiny sharp edged pieces of glas, the hesalite plastic plexi-glas of the Speedmaster Professional can break, but never disintegrate into shards. In micro gravitation shards can do any kind of harm imaginable. You can inhale them, it can be sucked into systems, cause tiny fractures in tubes and sealings and many other problems more. So the space watch needed to have a plastic glas. And that is a real weight saver as well.

Actually the Speedmaster is not really waterproof (just to 5 bars, what helps, when you wash your hands or get some rain). Neither the crown nor the pushers are screwed down to make them water tight. But as there usually is not so much water in space, let alone on the moon, so this was not an issue at all with NASA.

And if you don't take your Speedy for a swim, the missing screwed down crown is more of a feature than a bug. As it is a manual wind movement, you would have to unscrew the crown every one or two days to wind the watch. Missing that feature you actually just take it in your hands, wind it, period. No unscrewing the crown, winding and then screwing the crown back in. Just wind it, and it's ready to go.

A hand wound movement – is it a problem? Isn't that inconvenient compared to an automatic movement? Ok, first of all let's see it that way: wouldn't a quartz movement be even more convenient?

Let's face it: mechanical watches are for those of us who appreciate that whole conservative old-school, purely-mechanical, last-century timeless-beauty kinda thing. If you want to be efficient, modern and careless, buy a quartz Seiko. But if you wear your watch with consciousness, if you enjoy seeing it, feeling it, you probably will appreciate short intimate time with your watch, when you wind it.

Of course, a good automatic movement will never stop running if you wear the watch on a daily basis. If you only put it down for the night, you will probably over a course of ten or more years never need to unscrew the crown to wind the watch. And that is more than convenient, indeed it is quite cool, it's close to magic. Even a quartz watch needs a new battery every three or four years.

Is 42 mm too large and shouldn't I prefer the Speedmaster 'Reduced' that has everything that the Moonwatch lacks: convenient small 39 mm case diameter, automatic movement, sapphire crystal *and* transparent caseback to be able to see the movement in action, in short: everything you always wanted from your Speedmaster? So shouldn't I choose that one? In short: No.

Firstly I wouldn't never ever buy a product that is called 'Reduced'. Secondly every product that's not the original, the one-and-only, the icon, but as close to that as the Reduced, is just not the real one but a copy and for that reason simply uncool. Thirdly, the Reduced is not only *not* acredited for spaceflight (something every *real* guy needs as much as a chronograph), it wasn't for that reason not on the moon – and if that's a hoax – not even in earth orbit with the Space Shuttle – and probably with George Clooney.

No. The tenor is: get the real one and take pride in winding it like Buzz Aldrin did, before he stepped out of the Lunar Lander onto – well, at least some surface resembling the moon.

Enough of that. In reality all that is so important like James Bond wore a 5513 and Edmund Hillary made it to the Peak because he wore the Explorer. That is all nonsense that sells but when you have the thing on your wrist one thing counts more than that: is it cool? Is ist a beauty? Does it fit and does it wear with comfort? In one word: do you like it?

Truth is: the Speedy makes a great daily wearer. It wears light (as pointed out), it is versatile, it looks stunningly cool with whatever clothing you choose to wear (best with a suit), its readability and overall usability is quite good – and it is still a relatively cheap watch with a street price of \$3,500 retail, what I got it for.

And it is neither delicate not scarce as it is still in production and well available, so if you do break it, you don't destroy a endangered species, and you neither vaporize too much money – and this situation will probably never change until Omega goes out of business or NASA admits that they never went to the moon (whichever comes first).

The Beauty of Plexiglas

The Helsalite Speedy Pro crystal instantly makes you love vintage plexyglas watches.

Figure 12.2: Hesalite Crystal: Omega Speedmaster Professional

It is completely different from a sapphire crystal. Its round proportions and its plastic style mirrorings give it a very different

aesthetics than any glas crystal I know. So if you hear about someone praising his plastic Rolex models, there is definitely something
to it.

Weakness

The weakness of the Speedy is not its hand wound movement. That
is indeed not a problem at all. You get used to it very quickly. Its
weakness is the wonderful and beautiful hesalite crystal. Everytime
I cook in the kitchen I put the watch off, because I fear that a
spatter of hot frying fat could and would damage the plastic
plexiglas. And speaking of which: in practice you find that the
diving bezel of the Sea-Dweller is much better for timing your meal
in the frying pan than a chronograph. The diving bezel is just
perfect for it while the chrono is way too complicated and shows
way too much information that you just don't need – for cooking.

And there is another tiny issue with the Speedy: the seconds
hand of the chonograph. While the Speedy is basically perfectly
readable with its very classic white-hand-on-black-dial layout, the
white seconds hand of the chronograph (the running seconds hand
of the movement showing the time is the small seconds display at
9 o'clock) always stands at 12 o'clock and thus clutters the dial.
This is not a big problem, but while you can read a three-hands
watch with just one glance and a GMT hand usually does not
disturb you a bit, the very bright chronograph seconds hand of the
Speedy is a little bit in the way. Sometimes you with this would
be the time-seconds hand and the chrono's seconds hand would be
the small one at 9 o'clock. But this of course would make no sense
at all...

It is perfectly ok when you think about the use of the watch.
Think of it: being a precision instrument on the wrist of every
astronaut, its main purpose is measuring short portions of time
reliably with very high precision. The Speedy is not meant to show
what time it is in the first place, but to measure crucial timespans:
like e.g. the duration a rocket burns to bring a spaceship back
into earth orbit, especially when all other systems suck (like in the

Figure 12.3: seconds hand in the way: Omega Speedmaster Professional (2016)

Apollo 13 incident). And for that purpose the seconds hand of the chonograph is the most important hand of the whole watch, because this is the hand that shows that timespan with the highest possible precision. So if you use the Speedy as a daily wearer sitting on your desk or driving to a customer in your car, you just using it for the wrong purpose. That is not what it was meant for, although this original purpose is part of the heritage we love the Speedy for.

So we need to accept the watch as it is and complaining about the seconds hand is just a bit stupid.

My verdict on the Speedy:

Would I purchase the Speedy again? Definitely yes. Not only because my wife really likes it, I like it too. And it reminds me of the great deeds of people who fly into space and, ridiculously enough, makes me feel like I somehow was one of them.

State of the Collection

Now we come this far: we added another Omega icon and with that we not only got our first Moon-watch but our first chronograph in the collection.

Figure 12.4: added another icon: Omega Speedmaster Professional Moon-Watch

Chapter 13

What Rich People Do

You must understand one thing: To become, be and stay rich you must think and act like rich people do. They absolutely know why they are doing certain things, even if they don't tell everyone why. The first and most basic mistake poor people make is that they think rich people wouldn't act reasonable – basically because they themselves don't.

The first misunderstanding of poor people is, that rich people spend their money on whatever they want, because they have so much of it. That is the mindset of the lottery winner who is again as poor as before 12 months later, because he did not find anything better to do with the money than to spend it. Rich people are rich because they are pennywise. They don't make the mistake to think, a lot of money means to spend a lot, but they know: a lot of money means to save and invest it so that it creates even more money.

The truth is: poor people don't understand rich people at all. Rich people know exactly what the are doing. That is why they are rich in the first place. They know how to make money. And behind making money the second most important know how is how to save – not money – but value, buying power.

Poor people think, money is buying power and is to save. Rich people know, that money is of no value at all and must be exchanged into things of real worth.

The whole purpose of luxury goods is that they are extremely well made and durable, scarce, often even sought-after and hence they do keep their value for a long time. If someone pays a luxury price for something that looses its value like mid-tier consumer goods do (-50% the moment you leave the shop), he is either just out if his mind or obscenely rich – and probably won't stay rich over a longer stretch of time.

Luxury goods have another price courve like 'normal' consumer goods: first the price goes slightly down, when the thing gets older (like in the first 20 or so years of its existance) and then it again tends upward, because the thing becomes scarce and people tend to want it and so after 25 or 30 years price again goes up and now is again where it was in the beginning of the thing's existance – including inflation. So if inflation took you 50% of the value and buying power of your money on your bloody bank account and the luxury good 30 years ago was 10000 somethings (US-Dollars, Swiss Franks, Deutsche Mark or Euros – if that will last 30 years) after these 30 years of use and 50% of inflation this good is expected to bring you 20000 of these inflates somethings on the used market.

An interesting example for that sort of phenonenon is the market for used Porsche 911. If you look into it you find something very peculiar: a normal 20 year old used 911 is about 35000 Euros. A 30 year old one is 35000 Euros. And a 40 year old 911 is... well, 35000 Euros. That is the price curve of a luxury good when you calculate inflation and the initial retail prices into the equation.

A luxury good should always at least compensate inflation. Simply because it has an intrinsic value of its own. In the last 40 real years since about 1975 this funny theory was at least massively outperformed by the real world price develpment of e.g. Rolex steel sports watches. They did not only compensate inflation. Some grew by factor 10 or factor 100 – adding to inflation. You probably cannot expect that for the next 30 or 40 years from Rolex. But what you should still expect is inflation correction.

And in a full blown crisis like e.g. if an important currency should collapse, there will be a massive world wide run like a shock wave for stable values, like Gold, real estate and luxury goods that keep their value because they offer an important service (like telling the time) and will do this reliably for a very extended period of time because of their build quality. This could be quality luxury watches, luxury furniture, luxury houses, quality luxury cars, luxury beverages like high quality wine and whiskey, luxury musical instruments and of course precious metals like gold and silver. These things in such a situation will go up in price like rockets.

But: why of all things should the extremely expensive luxury goods keep and even increase their value in a crisis? Isn't that a very narrow and exotic market for some very few and very rich people? A narrow niche compared to the potent mass markets of the middle and lower class' products? And isn't build quality something very yesterdays? Shouldn't the mass products go up in price? Wouldn't that at least be fair?

No. In an economic crisis, not the rich become poor first but the poor become even poorer first. The whole system rotts from the bottom up. The poor first loose their cheap houses because the cannot pay debt any more from their small or in the probable case of unemployment completely absent income. So lots of cheap houses will be sold and begin to flood the market quickly, but find no buyers because no middle class people and of course no upper class rich people would ever buy a cheap poor peoples house. So the value of cheap houses crashes to nothing, zero, nada, immediately because there is lots of supply and no demand. What makes the poor people that still have their cheap house instantly completely broke also, because the probably only real value they possess, their cheap house, just lost all of its market value.

When the poor people are broken down completely, the middle class begins to erode from the bottom up by the same mechanism. That is because the middle class are basically poor people with more money. What they lack is the knowledge what to do with the money and how to make money – besides by being employed. Their money source is basically the same as the poor people's: employment.

The upper class people on the contrary aren't employed. They employ others in their companies. So it naturally takes a long time during which successively all their lower and middle class employees have to go, until their money machine ceases work.

Then, for the first time, the upper class gets in danger of loosing something.

The upper class is very stable. That is because the upper class has much more resources left before they fall into poverty and have to sell their (luxury) goods, what would affect the market for these goods. And that stability comes from the fact that they have their capital invested in stable and long lasting investments like real estate, company shares and luxury goods. Secondly, the upper class controls the economy and politics. Before they get in trouble as a whole, they change the rules so that others get in trouble instead. Thirdly, the upper class will eventually even profit from a crises.

And this always well-founded upper class will always look for goods that are suitable to store their capital, to be well equipped for every economic situation that may occur.

So even in serious trouble e.g. when a currency dramatically looses its buying power, when the poor usually loose all their money on their bank account and their job, while the rent for their flat rises, the rich by far don't get in trouble like the poor. The owner of the flat will still get the same buying power from them every month, the rent payment usually rises with inflation. The owner then, as fast as he can, tries to get rid of the nasty money to avoid loosing its value with inflation. What will he do? Of course he will look for goods he could purchase that do not loose their value, like gold, real estate and luxury goods – he will do that even more than in a normal economy!

So basically in a economic crisis everything the middle and lower class would buy, because they can only afford these things (or they are made to believe so) looses value dramatically because these people don't buy very much at all any more. As price comes from demand, prices for these goods fall – and so does their value on any used market. The lower and middle class people will try to save money so they basically stop consuming what destroys the value of all the things the usually would have bought. A massive oversupply lets prices drop like stones.

Only the rich still have buying power. They always try to make themselves independent from the stability of any currency. And so they buy what they always buy: expensive things of staying value.

With one word: they still buy luxury goods. Because buying luxury goods that keep value, as they are great quality and last very long, is not blowing money out of the chimney – what the poor think it was – but in truth storing value. The second truth here is: buying cheap means buying again, so in truth buying cheap indeed means blowing your money through the chimney.

The result is that even in a crisis, demand for luxury goods is still stable and while everything goes down, luxury goods become even more precious and sought after. And that again is why the rich stay rich. Because they are a subsystem of the market that uses other goods than the rest – high quality expensive long lasting goods – and for that reason do not suffer from economic crises, but even profit.

And that is why luxury watches keep their value not 'also' in a crises but 'especially' in one. And that is why you should do the same thing like the rich do: buy luxury goods like luxury watches. Because it's reasonable.

Chapter 14

Wrist Time

So now I took a little timeout. I could have gone on collecting these beautiful things, but I thought, take your time, don't hurry too much, perhaps first write a book about what you experienced so far.

And it is time to look at what watch is a good wearer, so let's look at the wrist time they get.

Wristtime is all about what you like, what feels good on your wrist and what is quite handy at the same time. And with a mechanical watch winding is always one of the issues that need to be dealt with.

Winding

Oftentimes people ask the question how you wind a mechanical watch. I don't know any 'right' way to do it, but I can tell how I for decades now wind my watches:

Automatic Watch

A automatic watch of course is self-winding, so in theory you never have to wind it, if you wear it everyday.

But that is the whole point. When we talk about collecting watches and you do not want to have your watches in a bank vault, but intend to enjoy them – what means wearing them – you will switch from one watch to another from time to time.

In the summertime e.g. you might wear a large specimen like the Panerai Luminor or the Hublot Big Bang, because it is fashionable, it is cool, large sports watches and military style watches are very en vogue. You wear a T-shirt with short sleeves and the size of the watch does not matter.

When sleeves are getting longer and the watch has to fit under a cuff, you perhaps switch to a smaller watch like the Rolex Explorer or the GMT Master II. And for Christmas the bling and the iced look of the Rolex Yachtmaster seems to be a very good choice. Also because its a bit delicate bezel is always perfectly protected under a winter sleeve or a cuff.

In the meantime all the timepieces you don't have on your wrist will cease working, after their power reserve is over after some 2 to 3 days. So when you put them on again, you no matter what also have to wind an automatic watch. And here is how I do it:

I unscrew the crown, pull it out completely, set the watch to the right time, push the crown one position in,

set the date (if it has one), and another position in,

wind it by rotating the crown with my fingers clockwise (this applies to Rolex movements). You feel how the movement is wound.

Then, when the seconds hand starts moving, I already stop winding (with a Rolex movement this should be after some 5 or 10 turns of the crown). This is enough power for the watch to keep running accurately from now on.

The rest of the winding up to maximum power reserve will be done by the self-winding mechanism. So I never fully wind my automatic watches by hand, but let the self-winding mechanism do the task. This works quite perfect for me. An advantage might be that you that way cannot damage the movement by winding it too hard.

There are things I do not do: some people again and again say, you wind the watch faster and more elegantly if you just let your index finger move back and forth under the crown, while it rolls on your finger. I do not like that, because you press the crown upwards doing that and that brings forces into the movement that don't belong there. I always use two fingers and the only force I apply is the rotation of the crown.

Handwound Watch

With a hand wound mechanical watch the thing is quite simple.

I unscrew the crown (in case of the Speedmaster this step is not necessary, as the Speedy has no screw-down crown, what makes winding so much more accessible and easy) and if the movement stood still you of course have to set the time and the date in the same way as with the automatic movement.

Then I wind to crown clockwise with two fingers, until I feel a slight some drag against the winding.

Then the movement is wound. I screw the crown back in. Ready.

Obviously you should do this daily. Even if you have more power reserve, it just is the easiest way to wind the watch every morning, when you put it on the wrist. If you do it let's say every second morning automatically the questions arises: did I wind it yesterday, or the day before...? And then you don't have complete control and in the worst case the watch stops, when you need that least. If you do it every morning, you know that you can rely on the power reserve, no matter what.

Additionally I think the movement works best, when the main spring is wound and offers maximum power.

Rolex!

A Rolex is the perfect amalgam of luxury and practicality. You can wear a Rolex basically everywhere anytime. It is rugged enough for mountain climbing, hiking and diving and classy enough for the night at the opera, a business meeting or just at a relaxed garden party with friends. With a Rolex you are never wrong. Not just because it is classy enough to wear it in classy situations, but especially because it is rugged and tool watch enough to also wear it in rougher moments, meaning, nearly every environment you can think of. It will not only do what it is supposed to do without complaining, it also can take one or the other blow.

This aura of practicality is different with other brands and watches. E.g. the Panerai Luminor is not so versatile. On the beach or in casual situations it is perfect, cool, modern, even trendy. But with a suit – not so much. The Omega Speedmaster is also quite versatile and goes with a suit as well as with a T-shirt. But would you wear a Speedy, even though it is water resistant up to 100 m in the pool? Not really. But the GMT Master, the Explorer, the Sea-Dweller, the Sub... Rolex just got it all right for every occation you can think of. Under water, up in the air, digging in a cave or racing a motorcycle – your Rolex will never let you down. And you feel that wearing the thing. I is reliable – more than you are.

On the Wrist or on the Arm?

The biggest unanswered question in luxury watches seems to be: where exactly do you wear your watch? I for one have no wrist time at all, as I do not wear my watches on the wrist. Hu? What-do-ya-mean? Here is what...

Sometimes when I look at wrist shots of people wearing their watches I downright get claustrophobia. And what I mean by that is clearly reflected in what these watches are called:

In English language they are called wrist-watches. Something that some people, mainly guys, seem to heavily missinterpret, what leads them to wearing the watch directly on their wrist, I mean litterally, exactly where the hand is joint to the arm. I completely cannot understand that. It hurts, it looks stupid and you probably cannot move your wrist around without the watch getting in your way. Wtf?

To show more clearly what I mean, let's in contrast have a look at the German word for wrist watches (sometimes the contrast to another language helps finding the true idea behind a specific wording). In German the idea of a watch you can easily access is described a bit differently: a wrist watch is called 'Armbanduhr' what basically means 'watch on a strap on the arm' If you translate it word by word: it is called an arm-strap-watch (Arm = arm, band = strap, Uhr = watch). Isn't German a cool language when you can say something so complex in just one short word?

Note that nobody says something about the wrist in the German word. Here the place to wear the thing is the 'arm' (obviously also in German nobody thinks about the bizeps, but of course the forearm). In German language and the according way of thinking derived from the words, such a watch is worn on the arm (not the wrist) held by a strap. So nobody even gets the idea of wearing a watch *on* the bloody wrist. It may slide down to the wrist, if you wear it loosely with a bracelet, but it is never fixed there. It basically is not meant to. Even if the 'wrong' or missleading word *wrist*-watch seems to suggest that.

And that quite reflects the difference how some people wear their watch. Some on the lower arm near to the wrist and some litterally *on* the wrist. I wear my watches on the arm (with a strap or a bracelet) not on the wrist.

Funny. Again a small example how language has the major impact on how we think and what we feel is right or wrong and what we therefore do.

By the way: the modern mobile watch, the pocket watch that eventually became the wristwatch – at first for women in the early 19th century lacking pockets, then for men, although they had pockets, in the early 20th century because they had to look at their watches regularly being a pilot or a solider in WW1 – this modern mobile watch was first invented in Nuremberg, Germany in the early 16th century. Many years later this industry settled in Switzerland and blossomed there in the very special and somehow peculiar way we know today as the Swiss Watch Industry

Perfect for...

Of course I wear my watches. That's what they are made for. But also I must admit, I wear them with caution. Because one thing I don't like: scratches and damage. I am not one of those only-a-watch-with-shards-is-a-real-watch guys, my 15 year old Omega Seamaster nearly looks like on the first day, although worn daily for over more than ten years.

That means, I simply take the watch off, when I do some hard work, carry something around, repair my bike or mow the lawn. That is no problem at all. I also do not do these things in a suit, so why shouldn't I take off the watch also.

However, although I love each of them dearly, some of them indeed do get more wrist time than others. and here is why.

In my case it is mainly a matter of comfort and usability.

Comfort and Feel

If I would have to put my watches into categories which of them sit with the most comfort on my wrist, it would be something like that:

10/10: Rolex Yachtmaster, Omega Seamaster Rolex GMT Master II

9/10: Rolex Explorer, Omega Speedmaster, Eterna Matic 1000

8/10: Rolex Sea-Dweller 4000,

7/10: Panerai Luminor

If I should give reasons for my choice of comfort it would be this:

- Rolex Yachtmaster: just absolutely perfect

- Rolex GMT Master II: perfectly balanced

- Omega Seamaster: near perfect

- Rolex Explorer: perfect, but a little too light

- Omega Speedmaster: a little light

- Eterna Matic 1000: very vintage small and the leather strap is a bit tight

- Rolex Sea-Dweller 4000: a little heavy

- Panerai Luminor: heavy and big

But this is not the whole truth. Comfort is not the only currency, a great feel on the wrist is payed in.

If you enjoy wearing either of this pieces depends not so much on the watch and its heft on the wrist, it depends primarily on your attitude.

If you expect a comfortable and easy to wear watch that you do not feel heavy on your wrist the whole day, you are probably wrong wearing a serious or even military style diver like the Rolex Sea-Dweller or the Panerai Luminor. Then you are probably better off with a Rolex Yachtmaster or the Omega Seamaster Professional. These wear light and easy and will not bother you in any way.

If you go on a vacation with a lot of sports and action, you will probably find the Rolex Explorer or the Eterna Matic too decent and dresswatch like – and the real dresswatch from Eterna too delicate. In such a situation you want a watch that not only forgives one or the other blow, you want a watch that gives you the feeling of the ruggedness. This is more like the Rolex Sea-Dweller or the Panerai Luminor. Watches that cry out for action and adventure to proof they are worth it.

If on the other hand you go to the office you might find the heft of a sports watch annoying. Then you are in a completely different mode and mood: you want a watch that suits you, that fits under your sleeve, that does not bother you throughout your workday that has plenty of challenges besides wearing a heavy and uncomfortable watch. You might even consider a watch that is iconic and stylish and decent at the same time like a Rolex GMT Master II, a Rolex Explorer or a Omega Speedmaster.

You of course can go on and on with that sort of considerations. But this is still not the heart of the matter.

If a watch sits perfectly on your wrist and fits you, depends not exactly on what you do, but on *how you feel.* If you feel masculine and your forearm is eager to flex its muscles and you feel like grabbing the next opportunity to win and be on top, if you feel really alpha male, a masculine watch like the Sea-Dweller, the Panerai or the Speedy feels quite right on your wrist. Its heft, its professionalism, its ruggedness, its will to go with you through every fight matches how you feel and what you expect from your little companion on your wrist right in that moment. You want to feel its weight and your ability to lift it and work with it. It is your companion and it should be every bit as tough as you are.

In another mood you might prefer a little less testosteron. Then you prefer a watch that sits a little lighter and more decent on your wrist. A watch that serves you more than it challenges you. A watch you enjoy by its elegance and brilliance, perhaps more for its looks and esthetics than its brutality. It doesn't matter if you are in the office at work or in a relaxed weekend. You don't need the proof of your physicality and masculinity, but you prefer the relaxed and laid back attitude. Even a little bit of bling and precious metals has its place in this mood and time. The the Rolex Explorer and the Rolex Yachtmaster might be your best choice here.

And if you feel like going to the dark side of the Moon, probably the Omega Speedmaster is your only right choice.

The new classic

The Omega Seamaster Professional is still a great wach. It does not look or feel outdated in any way or form. But I do not wear it so much, as it has one disadvantage: it became a classic and mine is still near mint condition.

So I basically can't wear it anymore! I don't want to risk spoiling it. Of course I wear it from time to time with pleasure as it still wears great and with perfect comfort.

...your favourite hobby

The Panerai PAM111 is not a watch for the office. It is a military watch (well sort of, to be honest it is just the Swiss homage to an Italian military watch from the 1940s) and for that reason it is hard boiled, rugged, brutal, sporty, provocative and very masculine. Silverster Stallone fitted quite well being their first 'ambassador' in the 1990s. And it's not much of a wonder that Arnold Schwarzenegger likes wearing them – besides his collection of AP Royal Oak Offshores, of course.

Figure 14.1: not for the office: Panerai Luminor Marina

So obviously it is a watch worth wearing in an environment with the same attributes. You can go swimming with it, or climbing, diving or river rafting.

Large watches like the Panerai Luminor or the Hublot Big Bang are cool in the summertime when you wear short sleeves. But in the wintertime, with cuffs and long arm shirts and stuff, large watches just suck.

So my PAM gets a lot of wrist time in the summertime, when sleeves are short and you can wear this big bloak of a watch on the wrist without colliding with cuffs or something.

The Panerai Luminor really feels masculine on the wrist. I

wear it with the black rubber strap, as I do not want to use and damage the brown leather strap, in case I ever want to sell the watch again. But that's just fine as the rubber thing wears way better than it sounds like.

It is a watch you wear like a muscle-strap around your arm, like weight lifters used to do and muscle-men in the old times. It gives you the feel that, if you flex your muscle, you could just bust that strap – even if you of course cannot. It looks best when you make a fist. It is the perfect watch for action and masculine fantasies.

So, what you find out is, you basically need at least a summer- and a winter-watch. The Pam is more like the summer-watch.

. . . everything with water

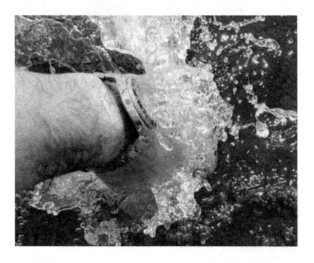

Figure 14.2: in its element: Rolex Sea-Dweller 4000

On the Mountain

The Explorer I was (well, sort of) on the Mount Everest, so it should be ok to bring it to the Alps, right? At least the Alps do not only resemble the Himalaya the way they look, they are of similar age and they even are brought into existence by the same mechanism: huge pressure from the south folded and still folds both up for about 40 Mio years now. Of course the pressure India does to Asia seems to be a lot higher, as the highest peaks of the Himalaya reach up to 8848 m and the highest of the Alps, pressured by the much larger African plate, only reach about half of that hight with the highest peak of about 4800 m. But heck, good enough for me.

Rolex advertised the Explorer saying that 'there is no watch-maker on a mountain', meaning, that this watch will not break in the worst moment or by the stress it gets climbing a mountain.

Figure 14.3: lightweight and elegant: Rolex Explorer 114270

So the mountains is its natural habitat. And wearing it there you find out that again lightweight is a real plus. It does not make so much difference under water (I estimate, as I did not bring my Sea-Dweller underwater), but it makes a big difference if you have to carry your watch up a mountain. Then, a bit like in flight or space missions, every little gram counts. And an unobtrusive and decent companion is very welcome.

Application for a Fake

I don't like my fake watch very much, as I already told you. But there are several occations I wear it nevertheless. Like riding the bike.

GMT Adventures

... but if you wear it every day, it is just a brillant, brillant, brillant watch.

For the first time I recognized the Rolex GMT Master II on the wrist of Formula 1 legend Nikki Lauda. That was back in the 1990s when Nikki Lauda was analyzing the Formula 1 races on TV. And this brought me to completely wrong assumptions about this watch.

I associated this very special watch with the blue and read bezel to racing and sports. And this seemed quite reasonable to me. The aggressive red, the dynamic clear blue somehow reminded me of typical colors at sports events. Red like Ferrari, blue like McLaren. It seemed obvious.

Obviously I did not understand that the GMT was a pilots watch. And as Nikki Lauda was a pilot and a airline owner he wore the GMT for the absolutely right purpose. And even being a business guy, who travelled the world and several timezones, he wore the absolute perfect watch for his lifestyle. But I basically did not understand that connection.

So to this day, the Pepsi GMT for me has a very sporty and very dynamic attitude. When I see it, when I wear it, I think of sports, pit chicks, racing cars and heroes in racing overalls risking their lives. And I feel like that when I wear it. And I don't feel like an airline pilot at all – although I should, if I only understood that thing I am wearing.

The Inlay

The GMT Master II 16710 – as we all know – comes in three flavours: Pepsi, Coke and Black. The Pepsi is very sporty and dynamic and classic at the same time - the Pepsi colored bezel is the genuine color combination Rolex started with the GMT in the 1950s. Later the Coke was added that is somehow a reduced Pepsi bezel where the vibrant blue is replaced by a much more defensive black. However Black and Red is also a very elegant combination. And then there is the Black, where the bezel looses its intuitive day/night function completely as it is just uniformly black.

This is by far the most elegant version of the GMT. While it at first might look a bit boring with its black on black on black 'color' scheme, it is indeed very classy and elegant and resembles of course the classic black on black Submariner. However it features the thin red line of the GMT hand and the 24-hour bezel which clearly sets it apart from the Submariner Date and makes it something more special.

So especially the Pepsi and the Black version of the 16710 GMT have their special attractivities. Of course the Coke and the later with the 6-digit ceramic era added Batman (blue and black) have their individual qualities, but in my humble opinion they don't meet the core of the GMT idea, but are just nice color variations.

So if you have the Pepsi GMT you will be quite happy in casual and sporty situations, but you begin to wish you had also a black bezel for the more formal occations. When you wear black, like black shirt and grey trousers or a black or dark grey business suit, the Pepsi bezel seems too colorful to fit that style.

The Cyclops

Things change. You adapt. You learn.

First you hate it. The Cyclops date magnification lens. You cannot think of anything but hating it. That ugly blob of sapphire over the date window. That unnecessary disturbance of the sapphire crystal's clear and flat elegance. That unnecessary magnifier for old people who can't remember what day it is. It destroys the looks of so many Rolexes. Watches that otherwise could be pretty.

Then you still hate it. And then you hate it even more. Even if you have it right on your arm, ontop of the watch you wear, the Rolex you actually wear.

And then... you someday... understand... you find out that... if something is indeed quintessentially Rolex... it's the Cyclops. There is nothing else more essential Rolex. Uach, sorry, gotta throw up...

Just kidding. Finally you love the Cyclops for exactly that reason. There is simply nothing more Rolex than the Cyclops. Rolex is a tool watch company. A Rolex is all about dedication. Usefulness. That they are popular, that they are beautiful, that they are cult is just a byproduct of... usefulness. And that also is the only point of the Cyclops: it is useful.

A watch without it may be a real Rolex with anything it needs, an Oyster case, a triplock crown, even with the laser rehaut... but it lacks something at the same time. Something essential.

Ok, Rolex did not use a lot of effort finding an attractive name for that quite unattractive thing. 'Cyclops'. Just say it a few times: Cyclops, Cyclops, CYCLOPS, cYcLOPS. Say it and try to like it at the same time. 'Cyclops'. There is simply not one association to this word that would be positive, even slightly advantageous. It lets you think of something huge, something nasty, a humanoid thing with one eye on its forehead. Lets you think of things quite unpleasant. 'Klops' (written with a k instead of the c) in german means something like meat loaf. This is all quite repelling. This is supposed to be part of a luxury watch, elegance, perfection, beauty, ... Cyclops ? On the other hand: the name fits this... 'thing'... quite perfectly.

At first I tried to avoid it buying a Sea-Dweller 4000 Ref. 116600, the only Rolex with a date but without the clops. Then I tried to ignore it on the Yacht-Master Ref. 116622. Then I wanted the GMT Ref. 16710 so badly that I would have bought it even if it had two Cyclopses. Then I was happy that the Explorer Ref. 114270 didn't have one anyway. And then...

And then I wore the 16710 for months. What a beauty, what an elegant and comfortable watch. Despite that Cyclops. And then I began to utterly like the Cyclops - wearing the GMT, on it, on top of it. You could recognize what kind of watch you were wearing by... the Cyclops on the crystal. How it reflects the light. How it thrones on the crystal, giving it character. Giving it purpose. No other watch has that.

And then I found myself thinking: perhaps I need a Sub Date with a Cyclops - because that is a Rolex! That exactly is a Rolex. The watch with the utter courage for uglyness. The watch that values toolness (and coolness) and practicallity over everything else. The watch that does everything possible for you to be able to read the date. The watch that even bears uglyness for you to be practical and toolish. A Rolex. No other watch would do that for you! With a Cyclops. A watch that gives everything for... you. Its wearer. Its owner. Its master. A watch hat sacrifices its beauty for your comfort. And that dedication, that utter selflessness in the end makes it even more beautiful.

That is a Rolex with a Cyclops lens.

Chapter 15

Where to go from here

If you think in terms of balancing your collection your choice gets reduced by the pieces you already have. All should make up a complete picture of... who you are?

But that reduction of choise is more a guiding light than a restriction. It tells you in your own inner logic and consequence what pieces would fit your existing collection best *now*. And that is of course always just an overlap with what watch you would like to own and wear.

You learn collecting, and collecting you learn. With each piece you own and wear, you learn more about watches and your next choice will be more competent and also be inspired by your last choices. But every choice gets easier, as you find out that other mothers have beautiful daughters also. You do not look for the one-and-only-perfect piece any more, but you enjoy the variety and the stories behind the watches, the stories of the watchmakers and the technological differences of the models and the brands. You 0.36become a collector and watch enthusiast.

Things I consider at the moment:

Rolex Submariner

First I thought about a Rolex Submariner nodate Ref.14060M from about 2010. I like youngtimers, because they are not accredited collectors choises – at least not yet. They are technically not worn out at all, some even are not worn very often by their first owner.

Figure 15.1: Rolex Submariner Ref. 14060 and 5513

Then I discovered the Submariner Ref. 5513 which was made from lo and behold! 1958 to 1989. It has the plastic crystal and the older models don't feature the whitegold support of the luminescent.

Rolex GMT Master II black Ref. 16710

Another model that sprang to my eye one day is the black on black GMT Master.

Figure 15.2: Rolex GMT Ref. 16710 black and coke with Jubilee bracelet

While this model line is dominated by the icon with the red and blue bezel (called Pepsi), and the other color combinations like the red and black (Coke) and the blue and black (Batman) just seem to be a mere variation of that original theme, the all black bezel version is different, it is very elegant, if you take a closer look.

Also the GMT in the coke version looks quite good with the Jubilee bracelet. This of course is very 1980s style, but I definite like it and perhaps end up with one of these to someday.

Rolex Daytona Ref. 16520

The last time I had the Daytona on my wrist I thought that it was too small. Too small. Says a guy who has an 114270 Explorer with the 36 mm case and *wears it*!

Figure 15.3: Rolex Ref. 16520 Daytona

Yes, and let me explain a bit why this is not a contradiction. It is not a matter of size, but of balance. The Daytona with the black dial and the steel bezel wears like a 36 mm watch. The dial looks like it was shrunk.

But the white dial version hasn't that sort of problem.

Rolex Daytona Ref. 116500

Sometimes things take a bit of time. After some months now, I still haven't seen the new ceramic Daytonas in reality.

Figure 15.4: Rolex Ref. 116500 Daytona (ceramic)

And for that reason, I still just cannot decide if I really like them or not. But what I can say is that I become more and more comfortable with their look. And so I will order one from my watch dealer in the next days. For the list price that is, what basically means that I probably won't get one within another 5 years from now. But that's ok for me. Good things take some time, sometimes.

Rolex GMT Master II 'Batman'

The same applies to the Batman. After you begin to ignore the broad shouldered Supercase you cannot resist finding the watch increasingly cool.

In the same way as with the new Daytona, Rolex changed the design of the GMT without really changing things. The designers changed the look and feel a bit, in order to make the watch look bigger and thus more connected to the design language of our times. But basically they did not change anything really. The numbers on the bezel now are larger, the case is a bit thicker around the

Figure 15.5: Rolex GMT Master II Ref. 116710 BLNR

waist, the hour indices are more emphasized than with the previous models. The ceramic bezel is a bit more present. But in truth: nothing really happened at all.

Besides of course the new and to this day unpreceded color combination BLNR (Bleu-Noire / Blue-Black) on the bezel. It even is the first multi-color ceramic bezel Rolex made. So there is also some technological significance to this model – if you dig that sort of thing.

It is a watch to have. A modern watch. And very cool. Just the right thing for you, if you drive a black Aventador. Like Batman would.

Rolex Explorer Ref. 1016

The 1016 also has the advantage of being produced over ages right until the early nineties. So there are also rather new ones with little wear available.

When you start dealing with watches, you may think, why on earth should I buy a watch with a plexiglas crystal, when there are ones the nearly indestructible sapphire available? And the reason you hear from collectors is: because the plexiglas is more beautiful. And tell you what: you don't believe them. It is plastic right? What has plastic to do with luxury in the first place and... until

Figure 15.6: Rolex Ref. 1016 Vintage Explorer

you see a plastic Rolex yourself. Then you know.

But this takes some time. The watch hobby is not one being conquered in a few days. And that is one of the beauties in it. You keep discovering new aspects and details for years, and that is not looking at the technological details of the movements at all.

No, probably not

These are watches I took into consideration but decided against them. Basically because I did not find them perfect. This is just my own personal impression.

Rolex Explorer II Ref. 16570

Now and then I try to like the Explorer II. But I cannot. I tried the white dial version with the result that I just don't like the black numbers on the steel bezel combined with the white dial (which itself is indeed beautiful).

Then I tried the black dial version and again, on the wrist it is a nice watch, but anotherone's nice watch. It somehow looks insignificant, somehow too busy but not really striking. Not for me.

Figure 15.7: not mine either way: Rolex Explorer II Ref. 16570

Perhaps I will try again, but the only Explorer II I find interesting is the old model from the 1970s, the 1657.

Tudor Black Bay Ref. 79220N

Sometimes I think, this hobby is too expensive. Let's get a nice watch for less money than minimum some 5 grand each time. Like the Tudor Black Bay 79220N, the Tudor hommage to the Tudor Submariner from 1960 which again is of course the cheap brother of the famous and today extremely expensive Rolex Submariner 5510.

It's a very beautiful watch. No question about that. On the worn out (looking) leather strap it looks gorgeous. Probably you learn to ignore the snowflake hour hand after some time. But that is the problem. . .

Is that Tudor an original watch? No it isn't. It's something like Rolex' inhouse fake watch of the James Bond Submariner 5510 from the 1960s. And I also do not like the brownish dial. Oh, of course I like how it looks. It is beautiful, no question about it. But it is not honest! It is a new watch that is made looking old – to meet the market needs of the vintage movement. It says: come and buy me because I look like what you are looking for –

Figure 15.8: Tudor Black Bay Ref. 79220N and Rolex Submariner Ref. 5510

but cannot afford. It is a fashion piece and that means it is not a focused tool watch that has its value in its own special qualities, but it is jewelry, like Hublot or even Panerai. And that means, it won't keep its value. Of course you can say, but also watches that are just timeless beauties keep their value. Perhaps. Perhaps it does. But it even it is not a real fake, like if Rolex would do it themselves, it is not the watch James Bond wore, it just *looks like that.* And that is a 'no', even if I come back to that model from time to time because I really like the looks and I'd really like to have a 5510. But I must keep up the discipline. it is still no.

And I never buy leather straps. Because they get damaged wearing them.

And coming back to the price: a watch for less than 5 grand isn't exactly a luxury watch (with some exceptions to the rule of course, like my Omega Speedmaster and the Omega Seamaster). And what am I doing here? Am I just having fun throwing money out of the window? No, I don't. I spend money on things that keep their value over long periods of time. Sometimes, very seldom, they even rise in value if you are very lucky. Normally they just compensate inflation, what is more than enough, when you think about which other things really do that trick.

I don't need another watch to just wear and have fun with. I am looking for value. And that's why the luxury segment is the only one I should be looking at, because the value-keeping phaenomenon is only there, and nowhere else. Everything else is just watches to find out what time it is.

Other than Rolex... seriously?

Of course there are also other watches than Rolex that appeal to me. But there are also of course not very many brands that should be chosen, as these all have a very louse resell value. So you of course can buy one of those watches, but they will not be in the same way as a Rolex be a means to store value over long periods of time. But if you are aware of that and if you go along with that (perhaps you have the purse to not really care at all), you'll be fine.

As sure as you need a chronograph, you need a pilot's chrono-graph. Just because it's cool, and of course because it's another one of the great watch genres you could feature in your collection.

Omega Speedmaster Mk II

Ok, it is not a huge step from Rolex to Omega. Omega is and was always a strong brand and a brillant manufacturer. With their Speedmaster, they even managed to beat the Rolex Cosmograph, later known as the 'Daytona', in their own little race to the moon. Well, as we all know, as everybody knows – the Omega marketing machine takes care of that – Omega made it to the moon while Rolex only reached a race track in the US.

And with the Speedmaster Mark II they of course tried to make everything even better. It got a date function, it went automatic (which of course is not appropriate for a space mission watch, as we discussed earlier), it got a very *very* 1970s tonneau case with an integrated even more spacey looking bracelet, that still today is beautiful and classy and vintage at the same time.

Figure 15.9: updated: Speedmaster Mk II

The Speedmaster Mark II is such a classic, that in 2015 Omega brought it back and presented a just slightly modernized version of the original 1970s watches. It of course is not the original and in that sense it is not the real thing, but a homage. But it has one major advantage: it is not 40 years old and worn but brand new.

Breitling Navitimer

Of course, you need to have at least one Breitling. And as Breitling is quite 'special' in its aesthetics, this is not an easy task especially, if you prefer more decent, subtle, quiet and smaller watches. Because all of that is Breitling not. Breitling is big, loud and show-off in essence.

But one thing is true: *You can't say anything against the Navitimer.* Breitling's Navitimer indeed plays in the same league as the Submariner, the Speedmaster and the Daytona. It is an icon. If the Speedmaster is the iconic Moon-watch the Navitimer is the iconic Pilot's watch. From the old days of course. Because today nobody needs a round sliderule on his watch to calculate is approach speed.

But all of that is heritage and dedication, of course. And if you want a *smaller* more classic watch, you of course can choose the classic 43 mm version.

Figure 15.10: one more icon: Breitling Navitimer 01

But what I do not want, even if this is the original Navitimer configuration, is the Navitimer with the Valjou 7750 movement. But these days Breitling makes very good inhouse movements and this seems to be the way to go.

That's why I also here don't think about a vintage model, even if it might be a more original one, as this watch is like the Speedy in essence a vintage piece. It's an old watch that nobody today really needs, to be honest. But it's cool.

And in this single watch I would take the leather strap version even if there is a metal bracelet – just for the looks, and because it is the classic pilot's configuration. At 20.000 ft and -10 °C you just cannot wear a metal bracelet on your wrist, because it would basically freeze off your wrist.

IWC Big Pilot

The IWC Big Pilot is a reminiscence to the large pilot's watches of the 1950s and 1960s. It indeed is smaller than its predecessor: the Big Pilot is 46 mm in diameter – the original pilot's instruments of that forgone era was 55 mm. So the Big Pilot Heritage model comes with 48 mm oder 55 mm diameter. Historically accurate, but to wear it under a cuff?

Figure 15.11: rather big: IWC Big Pilot and beautiful, Big Pilot Heritage

Why I won't buy one: they are too big to wear them regularly. Yes, you can put them on, it is fun and really impressive. But in the long run? I tested the 44 mm form factor with my Panerai Luminor and my Big Bang Fake and my verdict is clear: these big watches are not comfortable to wear.

And that is, because in the case of the pilot's watches, they have never been meant to be comfortable. They are meant to work. To function. They even aren't exactly luxury watches, but extremely perfectionized and therefore expensive tool watches. There is a reason why they are so big: because they are aviation instruments, they need to be readable in any kind of stress situation. That is why they have big readable dials. And they need to be handled easily even with gloves on, so they have large, oversized handles. That is all quite reasonable if you are a fighter pilot. If you are a office fighter, these things make less sense. Indeed they reduce the fun you can have with such a watch, when you cannot wear it together with a cuff. So, if you like that kind of uncomfort, go for it, I know, that comfort is important for me, so I will probably continue admiring these watches from a distance.

And there are two more problems: firstly, they come on leather straps. So I need to buy them new, because you cannot clean a leather strap like a bracelet. Second, the price is not too modest. IWC is not a company famous for their mild pricing policy. These Big Pilot watches are about $10,000 new, which is something you have to intend to invest in a watch that will only somehow keep its value over the years.

Hublot Big Bang

The Big Bang is a sort of hybrid between a classic and a true fashion watch. It is a rather individually designed watch with at rather standard ETA movement. It is rather luxurious and pricy and comes with a rubber strap. Jean Claude Bivier, the godfather of Hublot says: »Yes, of course we are crazy«. And he is right. They are.

Figure 15.12: cool styling: Hublot Big Bang, BB Evolution and BB Unico Ceramic Black Magic

Nevertheless, I still fancy the Big Bang. And especially the Unico versions with the 'inhouse' movement that Hublot bought from a movement development company and the black ceramic casing, that is quite light and easy to wear.

I always fancied the skeltonized Big Bang, called Aero Bang. And I once tried a Big Bang Black Magic on my wrist and it a bit

like sat there on my wrist to stay. So light, so comfortable, so...
black. And so this seems to be my Hublot dream watch: the Unico
Black Magic, light to wear, because it is ceramic and on the other
hand the brillant design and Hublot's characteristic provocative
style.

To me the whole black on black on black case thing looks like
a protection surrounding the open inner heart of the watch that is
visible trough the crystal. It is like a stronghold of like military
strength around that very delicate and stripped inner core.

And on a much more basic level, the ceramic is just very
comfortably light – a good thing for a 45 mm watch. In steel this
size would tend to unwearable. But this one... (sigh)

Even farther ahead...

Do I dare precious metals, high horology or even Holy Trinity?

JLC Deep Sea

The watch with the longest name in watch making history. The
'Jeager LeCoultre Master Compressor Chronograph Deep Sea'. You
cannot get any more precise than that.

Yes, also Jaeger-LeCoultre has a 'Deep Sea', one other than the
famous Rolex bigfish is actually wearable and indeed very pretty.

It has just one problem: JLC has not the market standing that
Rolex has. Nobody knows them, and so prices are not as stable
as Rolex prices are. While the retail price of the JLC Deep Sea
is $10,000, you can find them on the internet for just $7,000 new.
Doesn't seem to be a good fellow in terms of value for money.

And that's a pity because it is really a brillant, beautiful watch.
With the leather strap and the black bezel it looks very classy and
you either can wear it with a suit or you can go swimming with it.

Figure 15.13: JLC Master Compressor Chronograph 'Deep Sea'

Audemars-Piguet Royal Oak

The AP RO. Of course. The 'Royal Oak' – silly name for a watch, isn't it?

What on earth made the Royal Oak Company, pardon, Audemars-Piguet call its groundbreaking 1970s model Royal Oak? Is it royal? Moreover, is it an oak?? No! It's a watch! Truth is: the Royal Oak was a ship, a boat, a famous yacht!

Figure 15.14: AP Royal Oak Ref. 15202 and Royal Oak Chronograph Ref. 23000

Audemars-Piguet, runner for number one for the most unpronounceable brand names in the watch market. AP, the great. AP the holy trinity member. AP, in classic order number two behind Patek. But is that so? I somehow get the impression, that the real number one of todays watch market is AP. Of course it used to be Patek and in the much less expensive luxury segment it definitely is Rolex. But beyond the luxury segment?

If you look at the high horology, the haute horology sector, where there is the hol trinity Patek, AP and Vacheron, and besides that happens to be Jaeger-LeCoultre, A. Lange from Germany and perhaps Blancpain and Breguet, you find that something has changed over the years. And that is that a decent man does not any more have to wear a dress watch. He can pull off a sports watch to a suit!

Of course Patek is the Rolls Royce of them all. But does that mean that everyone has to drive a Rolls? Perhaps this similarity of the brands goes a bit too far: also Patek seems to me a bit stuck in their own grandessa. They seem to do a lot technologically, inside the movement. But in terms of models?

They all seem to me a bit old men's models. They don't really pop, obviously because they shouldn't in the first place. Patek makes very very decent watches. However, this is all a bit boring. And since the border between dress watches and sports watches vanished and every sports watch is also wearable as a dress watch, the whole point of a decent dress watch is gone.

And here it is, the time of the rebels, the misfits, the big, the provoking models. Even today's top celebrities and aristocrats don't wear Patek any more: they wear AP.

So the question must be allowed if the new king really is the old king or if things just changed.

Patek Nautilus Ref. 5711

Finally, we would enter the crown of it all, the top brand, the finest of the finest, the most renown and the most heavily priced: Patek Phillippe.

Figure 15.15: Patek Phillippe Nautilus Ref. 5711

The Nautilus is in my opinion something like the crown-jewel of every collection. Of course there are more expensive watches and there are many other nice ones. But not very many are as brillant as the Nautilus.

Chapter 16

Recommendations

We of course would also recommend to you the following ebooks...

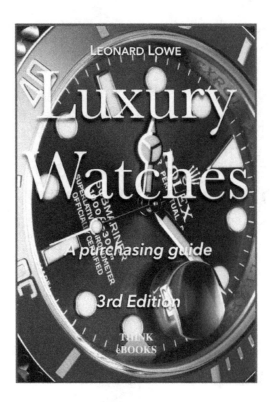

Luxury Watches – A Purchasing Guide

A luxury watch is more than $5,000. So naturally in this topic there is a lot of money involved. This book will help you to avoid wrong decisions that would cost you huge amounts of money. It will help you to understand how the luxury watch market works. There are a lot of watchmakers and even more watches on the market. It will help you to identify the top brands and watches that not only look nice, but are a good investment into the future. Vintages models are very en vogue for some years now. So if you consider purchasing a luxury watch, there are a lot of things you need to know. Like e.g. What is a luxury watch and what makes it so expensive? What models and brands keep their value over years, which even grow in value? What are the top watch brands of the world? What are the top watch models, the timeless classics available? Should I buy a replica watch? Can a luxury watch be a financial investment like artworks, oldtimers or precious metals? This book will help you with basic knowledge and some personal advice.

Please find links to this book at all the major ebook stores as well as the paperback edition at

http://www.think-ebooks.com/luxury-watches/

Rolex Watches

5/5 Stars ***** Well worth reading and at a fair price: »This is a very useful and clearly written primer for anyone who is interested in Rolex watches. All of the modern and many of the vintage watches are covered. The compact format is a handy feature.« (Harrell, March 4. 2017)

5/5 Stars ***** MUY BUENO.« (Juan Carlos Camino, March 15. 2017)

This ebook provides a lot of purchase relevant background information on the most important Rolex models. With this ebook you will be able to select the watch you want to purchase with ease. You will have a quick overview of the Rolex models and understand why they are there and why some models are considered more important and valuable than others.

The Rolex lineup of watches evolved over time. And like every naturally evolving structure it is a bit confusing at the first and often also second look. It helps a lot to understand when and why which model was introduced and what changes it got over time. You also will be able to understand the Rolex vintage collectors' movement, that values old Rolex models much higher than the modern lineup.

This ebook tries to sort this out a bit. To understand what watch is meant for what audience, what differences are there between the models, and how the whole thing did evolve since the 1950s, this book will give you some important advice.

It is no question if you will find the best watch for you within the Rolex world, if you just know the details we present to you in this ebook. And selecting the right Rolex is always a matter of money. So be wise and learn, before you buy.

This is not a Rolex sales catalogue. In contrary to such an approach we tried to cover all the information that is not given on official websites but nevertheless should make it much clearer, how the Rolex models are connected to each other and what might be the right one for your wrist.

Links to (purchase) this book are here:

http://www.think-ebooks.com/rolex-watches/

Ten fun Things to do with Luxury Watches

A book not only about collecting watches...

Ten fun things you can do with luxury watches... well, ok, it ended up being thirteen things, not ten. But that already says a lot. And no, it not only says that you get 30% more than you payed for... it says something about watches, about having watches as a hobby and about the fun you can have with them. Because basically it is always fun to deal with something beautiful, with something perfectionistic and with some piece of art. It means dealing with something higher than you are and that alone lifts you up.

A luxury watch is not just a watch. You can do a lot of smart, fun and interesting things with a watch, inspired by a watch or in companianship with a watch.

This ebook will give you some ideas, inspiration and even reason, why some people are interested in these very special watches and often frantically collect them. Keep in mind: we are talking about watches that are 'defined' by these peculiar characteristics: they are made in Switzerland and they are at least $5000.

Of course there is more to a 'real' luxury watch than these two base characteristics. A lot of people narrow the whole industry that consists of dozens of companies down to about 9 really important companies: Rolex, Omega, Breitling (that much about the companies you probably already heard about) and there is Patek-Philippe, Audemars Piguet and Vacheron Constantain, who are called the Holy Trinity (!) and there is Jaeger-LeCoultre, Breguet and IWC, who are... well... also very important. For a first take you can ignore all the others. Perhaps you will encounter Hublot and Panerai and other brands that try to distinguish themselves from the mainstream. They can be entertaining too...

Watches are a really rewarding hobby. You can do a lot of things with watches and around them. They are a kind of technology that is around for about 300 years and the oldest companies in the market are nearly there from the very beginning. So you can learn a lot about very different areas on this very peculiar, very special and very secluded market: about luxury of course, also about style, about beauty, about technology, about marketing, about riches and rich people, about capital, money and lasting value, about time and timelessness, about fun and application, about diving, space travel, precision measurement and last but not least about the biggest secret of them all: about time.

So let's have a little stroll around and look what watches have got in for you. There is something that you will find interesting or even inspiring. Trust me and come with me for a few precious moments together...

Please find links to this book at all the major ebook stores as well as the paperback edition at
http://think-ebooks.com/ten-fun-things-to-do-with-luxury-watches/

Tell us Your Opinion

Thank you very much for reading this ebook. We would of course very much appreciate if you liked the ebook. If you have any further questions on the subject, have some criticism or ideas for improvement please feel free to tell us your thoughts: please write to leo.lowe@rocketmail.com or visit our website at THINK-ebooks.com

9 783739 383675